INVISIBLE HEROES

OF WORLD WAR II

Also by Jerry Borrowman

Beyond the Call of Duty

Compassionate Soldier

INVISIBLE HEROES

HEROES

OF WORLD WAR II

Extraordinary Wartime Stories
of Ordinary People

JERRY BORROWMAN

SHADOW
MOUNTAIN

Visit us at shadowmountain.com

Library of Congress Cataloging-in-Publication Data
Names: Borrowman, Jerry, author.
Title: Invisible heroes of World War II : extraordinary wartime stories of ordinary people / Jerry Borrowman.
Description: Salt Lake City, Utah : Shadow Mountain, [2019] | Includes bibliographical references and index.
Identifiers: LCCN 2018039673 | ISBN 9781629724171 (hardbound : alk. paper)
Subjects: LCSH: World War, 1939–1945—Biography. | Heroes—United States. | Heroes—France. | LCGFT: Biographies.
Classification: LCC D736 .B67 2019 | DDC 940.84/12730922—dc23
LC record available at https://lccn.loc.gov/2018039673

Printed in the United States of America
Publishers Printing, Salt Lake City, UT

10   9   8   7   6   5   4   3   2   1

This book is dedicated to the men and women of the United States military, as well as the families who support them, for the sacrifices they make in fighting for the cause of freedom—and particularly to those who have achieved great things despite discrimination and prejudice.

War is an ugly thing, but not the ugliest of things:
the decayed and degraded state of moral and patriotic
feeling which thinks nothing worth a war, is worse. . . .
A man who has nothing which he is willing to fight
for, nothing which he cares more about than he does
about his personal safety, is a miserable creature, who
has no chance of being free, unless made and kept
so by the exertions of better men than himself.

—JOHN STUART MILL, *THE CONTEST IN AMERICA*, 30.

CONTENTS

AUTHOR'S NOTE

Each of the chapters in this book shares inspiring stories from World War II. Some include additional incidents from other wars and military conflicts to more fully develop the theme and provide context. All of the chapters are about heroes—some are individual profiles, others are about groups of men and women who often serve out of sight but never out of danger.

It is an honor to bring these stories to light so that the bravery and sacrifices of so many people offered in behalf of freedom are recognized.

PART ONE

INDIVIDUAL HEROES

CHAPTER 1

PAT PATTON

ABANDONED AT BATAAN

The story that follows comes from personal interviews with Henry Robert "Pat" Patton, a survivor of the infamous Bataan Death March and prisoner of war in Japan during World War II. I took detailed notes during our interviews and then wrote the story in first person, doing my best to capture Pat's voice and manner of expression. Pat reviewed the text to make sure it captured his thoughts and memories accurately and, before his death in March 2007, gave permission to have this account published.[1]

Pat escaped the entirety of the Bataan Death March by fleeing into the jungle with a friend. He then helped organize a guerrilla campaign against the Japanese until his ultimate capture and imprisonment. Eventually, Pat was transferred to Japan as a slave laborer to work in the coal mines, where he suffered terrible physical privation and inhumane mental and emotional abuse. He witnessed the deployment of and destruction caused by the first atomic bomb, dropped on Hiroshima. As a prisoner of war, he was an invisible soldier. And, like the other soldiers captured in the Philippines who lived through the greatest defeat in American history, Pat returned to a country that was largely indifferent to his suffering.

Still, the survivor instinct that kept him alive when more than 30 percent of the Americans taken prisoner by the Japanese in the Philippines died, saw him through the rest of his life. His is one more witness of the indomitable human spirit that allows a person to survive and triumph over great horrors and persecution. Like the other American and Filipino soldiers who fought valiantly for freedom in the face of insurmountable odds, Pat is a hero.

A MEMOIR OF BATAAN

"I grew up in Nebraska during the bleak years of the Great Depression, famous in history for the dust bowl that devastated our crops and filled the dusty skies with centuries of precious topsoil. Like many others, our family felt the effects of the creeping poverty afflicting American farmers and their families. Perhaps it was the anxiety and insecurity of those times that encouraged my mother and me to fight so much, but the truth is I was anxious to get away from my home just as soon as I could (my father died when I was just twenty months old). When war broke out in Europe, I figured that a draft couldn't be too far away, and I much preferred to choose my own way of serving, so I enlisted in the Army Air Force in 1940. The Army was my ticket to freedom; to get as far away from Nebraska as possible, I signed up for overseas duty. After basic and specialist training, I was assigned to the Philippines in March 1941. That was about as far away as I could get. My specialty was as a radio operator aboard military aircraft.

"In 1940, the Army really didn't understand the military potential of an air force. Most of the generals in Washington thought it was nothing more than a battlefield gimmick that had some value in providing intelligence to ground troops but little practical application in battle. Their experience in World War I was that most air combat had been between the aircraft themselves, and that the occasional bomb dropped over the side by a pilot had little effect on the ground battle. But by 1941, the range, speed, and power of aircraft had expanded considerably, and the war in Europe was showing just how important this new technology was to the total war effort. Still, the staunch isolationist movement at home made it difficult for the Army or Navy to get funds to invest in airplanes. The effect was that the Army had very little functional equipment at the outbreak of the war. That was certainly true in the Philippines, where we had a handful of obsolete observation aircraft and a few small bombers and fighters. At most, we had about ten to eighteen operational bombers at Nichols Field. I was assigned to the Second Observation Squadron, where we trained on a Curtiss O-52 observation aircraft and Douglas B-18 bomber.[2]

"Most of us really enjoyed our service in the Philippines. It was oppressively hot in the winter months, but the lush vegetation and tropical setting was a perfect contrast to the drab Nebraska plains I'd wanted to get away from so badly. Plus, I enjoyed having lots of friends around all the time, and, with no battles raging, we had plenty of time for rest and relaxation when not on duty. The threat of war was ever present, and all the experts figured that if we did engage the Japanese, the Philippines would be the first place attacked. Military planners assured us that they had laid in a six-month stockpile of food and ammunition, and that a Japanese attack on Manila would inevitably fail because of the big guns located on the island of Corregidor in the mouth of Manila Harbor. And even though we were thousands of miles from America, the Pacific fleet stationed in Honolulu, Hawaii, could easily reach us before the Japanese could mount a full invasion. So even though we were in a dangerous place, we weren't really too concerned. Plus, being young and naïve, we were actually kind of excited to get into battle and to experience the thrill of combat. It's hard to imagine now that we could have been so stupid.

"Monday, December 8, 1941, dawned like any other. We'd had a lazy Sunday the day before, listening to American music on the shortwave radio, spending time at the enlisted club, and playing cards. Rumblings between Japan and the mainland had put us all on an increased alert for the past several weeks, but as each day passed with nothing happening, we had let our guard down and figured it was just more political maneuvering.

"This calm serenity was shattered shortly after I rolled out of bed when someone came in shouting that the Japanese had attacked Hawaii just five hours earlier. Everyone at Nichols Field ran to the radio hut to listen in, and we were stunned to hear that the Japanese had somehow mounted an all-out attack on the Pacific fleet and that they had destroyed or disabled nearly all the battleships and destroyers that sat moored in their berths in Pearl Harbor. Suddenly we were sick to our stomachs. This wasn't the way it was supposed to happen! The fleet was our only connection to America, and if it was out of action, we were all alone in the middle of the vast South Pacific.

"A friend and I rushed to the runway and climbed aboard an old observation aircraft to get up in the air to see just what we were up against. What we saw was enough to shake even a battle-hardened soldier, let alone two new recruits who had never seen hostile action. Japanese warplanes filled the skies, heading straight for us. Our goal was to feed information to our ground-based troops to help them respond to the air attack and to find shelter, when necessary. Unfortunately, our flight was short-lived, as we were shot down just a few minutes after takeoff. Our puny little plane was nothing compared to the Japanese Zeroes, which could fly higher, faster, and with greater maneuverability. We managed to parachute to safety without serious personal injury and went up a second time. Sure enough, another fighter found us and shot us down. By the end of the next day I might have set a record in aviation warfare: I'd been shot down three times in two days! That pretty much put an end to my flying career, as all of our aircraft had been destroyed. After losing our aircraft, we were designated as the Provisional Air Corps Infantry.

"When the Japanese landed ground-based troops, they began a systematic advance through the island. Facing air superiority of 200 to 1, there was little the Allies could do to prevent the fall of Manila. Our contingency plan called for retreating American and Filipino troops to hold the defensive lines as long as possible and then to retreat toward the Bataan Peninsula west of Manila. By doing so, our forces would become ever more concentrated and more difficult to dominate. On Christmas Day, 1941, just eighteen days after the initial assault, we received orders to withdraw to the peninsula. Once all troops were there, we formed up defensive lines, with a large mountain in the center. Being so hopelessly outnumbered was quite depressing, but the Marines I was with fought with distinction, inflicting serious damage on the Japanese units that came against them. We made the Japanese earn every inch of ground and did our best to harass and delay their advance. Little did we know that in doing so we were setting ourselves up for even more brutal treatment after their ultimate victory. The truth is that the Japanese thought they could conquer the Philippines with little effort, and our stubborn resistance infuriated them.

"As the battle lines shortened and we backed further down the peninsula, the lack of planning by the general staff became apparent. We'd always been told that there was a six-month supply of food and ammunition; but it was either a lie, or all the supplies were stored safely on the island of Corregidor, where constant harassment by enemy aircraft made it difficult to get supplies over to the peninsula.

At any rate, we were first put on half rations, then third rations. We lived in constant hunger from a diet of fewer than 800 calories per day while expending all our physical effort to fight back the Japanese. This malnutrition made us far more susceptible to tropical diseases, and soon most of the troops were both hungry and sick. All the local snakes and other wildlife were consumed for food. Still, we fought with everything in our power to beat back the Japanese.

"Perhaps one incident describes what had become of us. One night, as we settled in for darkness, we heard the Japanese shouting 'Tonight you die!' which may have been the only English words they knew. Sure enough, a huge battle broke out later in the night as they charged our position with their famous *banzai* cry. We had done a good job of digging in, and when the morning broke we climbed out of our foxholes to find more than 300 Japanese dead. It was an appalling sight, but we hardly had the energy to care or even notice. Someone mounted a large bulldozer and carved out a huge trench. Just as we were ready to start throwing the bodies in, one small American soldier cried out, 'Isn't somebody going to say something!' That's when it hit us just how battle-hardened we'd become. Everybody went quiet, and one of the officers moved to the edge of the trench and said a few words about this being the last resting place for these men and calling on God to receive their souls. At that, the little guy broke out in sobs. I saw seven or eight guys go over and put their hands on his shoulder to comfort him, and for at least a few moments we remembered our humanity. It hadn't been destroyed yet—just buried under months of hunger, fear, and vicious fighting.

"The original purpose of a withdrawal to Bataan was to allow for the systematic evacuation of troops if a general retreat was ordered. But with no navy to provide ships, the only people to evacuate were General MacArthur and his family and staff. In March 1942, this small group boarded four small PT (patrol torpedo) boats, overloaded with gasoline, and managed an escape to Australia.[3] By this time, we had come to hate the Japanese because of the viciousness they displayed when capturing Allied troops. We all knew that it would be better to die in combat than to be taken prisoner. Plus, we all felt an obligation to fight to the last man, if necessary, to defend our country's honor.

"The group of Marines I was with was committed to staying in the battle to the end, which is why it was so galling when we were ordered to surrender in April 1942. Many Marines simply refused to obey the order, but it didn't matter in the long run because there was no place to escape from the now-victorious Japanese. The night before the surrender, orders were given to torch all the gasoline and equipment in the southern end of the Bataan Peninsula so it couldn't be used by the enemy. Fires illuminated the night sky in a scene that looked like everything I'd been told about hell. The Japanese continued to fire on us even though our surrender was imminent, so there we were—sick, hungry, and under fire while watching our only means of resistance go up in flames. I could not imagine a more depressing sight.

"It was probably a noble gesture to burn the equipment, but in the end, it only hurt us. If the trucks had been left, the Japanese would have used them to transport us to our prison camp. However, since the equipment was gone, they ordered us to march. Just imagine nearly 70,000 men filing onto a dusty, rocky road with no food, water, or other provisions, under guard by an enemy that despised them. The Bataan Death March would cost thousands of human lives in just five days.[4]

"When the Japanese saw how many prisoners they had to care for, they were quickly overwhelmed. If they had any plan or organization, it wasn't apparent. They'd shout at us in Japanese to do something, and when we didn't understand they'd clobber us with the butts of their rifles. In more than one case, I saw them simply shoot an offending prisoner. It didn't matter to them that we couldn't speak Japanese. In their minds (and in ours too), the ultimate humiliation was to surrender, and in doing so we gave up whatever rights we might have otherwise been entitled to. As I learned more about the Japanese in the next three years, I came to understand that they believed that theirs is a divine race, brought down from heaven by the Sun God, and that the rest of the world was inferior to them. Because their island was so isolated, none of the soldiers who became our guards had any experience with other cultures, and so they regarded us as completely worthless.

"The acts of cruelty on the march were just too much for me. I couldn't stand how they treated people, yet I knew that if I showed any resistance, or even tried to help an American, they'd turn on me in an instant. The only thing I could think of was to slip off the road and try to hide in the jungle. At just the right moment, when no guards were looking, my friend Donald Stratton and I quietly disappeared into the Philippine jungle. If the Japanese had found us, it would have meant instant death. Fortunately, we lost ourselves in the thick undergrowth and hid out long enough for the column to move out of sight. We then found refuge with several Filipino families in nearby villages.

"At first, we were in no condition to do anything except cling to life. From May to September, both of us were overcome by malaria and spent our days and nights suffering from the high fevers and chills that characterize this disease. The Filipino families that cared for us used local remedies to help fight off the fevers. I'm convinced that without their help I would have died. There were many days when I was so sick that I didn't know why I wanted to live. But somehow I did and therefore clung on to life as best I could.

"Eventually, we had to move because the Japanese had begun harassing Filipino families suspected of harboring the enemy. Oh, the things we saw the Japanese do to the Filipino women—raping and torturing and then killing them with no thought or remorse! Japanese soldiers found horribly creative ways to make the Filipinos suffer and found perverse pleasure in their total and unchallenged authority. I could never have imagined that any human being would do what they did to another person, particularly because I knew the Filipinos to be such kind and loving people. When they were done with the women and children, they always killed the men, and whole villages were burned to the ground. The suffering was unimaginable, and I could never knowingly put a family at risk for our benefit, so we moved out into the jungle.

"The Japanese were more experienced soldiers than we were, but they didn't have anywhere near the background in stealth and stalking of a couple of guys who grew up hunting for game in the Midwest. More than once I hid just a few feet from a Japanese patrol, and they never had any idea. As we regained our strength, we decided to move up into the mountains to try to find any other refugees to join up with. Prior to the war, two German brothers had owned a large plantation which they had since converted into a guerrilla base station. It was nicknamed Fawcett's Camp, and it became my home for the next year. It was so great to be around other Americans. Together we managed to find enough game and produce to start rebuilding our shattered health. One of the things that really helped is that we created a makeshift hospital.

"Dr. Pineda, a Filipino, volunteered at the hospital and saved many American lives. If the Japanese had found him out, they would have tortured and killed him with no remorse, which means he literally put his life on the line to save us.

"Unfortunately, there were few medical supplies to help fight off the local diseases, so a few of us decided to venture out into the country to see what we could find. Our plan was for some of us to conduct a guerrilla campaign to disrupt Japanese control, while the others found food and whatever supplies they could. I organized a group of forty to forty-five Filipinos to go out on these raiding parties—eventually my group included sixty-two guerrillas! Our first guerrilla action was rather gruesome but certainly had the desired result of upsetting the Japanese. One of the local scouts had spotted a place on the main road where the Japanese moved troops on a fairly regular basis. He suggested that we stretch a wire across the road at the level where the Japanese troops stood in the back of the truck. A few of the locals, who could move in and out of town without being discovered, cut a guy wire off a hotel. Meanwhile, another group scouted out a narrow spot in the road where the jungle closed in. At the narrowest point, it was eighty-two feet from tree to tree. On a day of low Japanese traffic, the Filipinos strung the wire, placing it a few inches above the top of the cab of a typical troop transport vehicle. Two men stayed to watch while the rest of us went back to the hills. In the late afternoon, a truckload of Japanese soldiers barreled down the road at full speed. Sure enough, most of them were standing in the back of the truck when it passed under the taut wire. Eight of the troops were decapitated and killed instantly, with even more wounded. The truck drivers had no idea what had happened, so they drove nearly a mile down the road before the survivors in the back were able to get them to stop. The medical need was so urgent that they didn't retrace their path to find where our wire was hidden. The next day, another truck went through the spot, and twenty-two Japanese were killed. A third truck figured out what was happening, found the wire, and destroyed it. Needless to say, the Japanese were furious and carried out reprisals against the local people, but to our knowledge none of them were killed. It may not seem like much, but after everything the Japanese had done to both the Americans and Filipinos, it was a symbolic victory that made us feel like we were doing something to help the war effort. To the degree that the Japanese had to keep more troops occupying the Philippines, they would have a smaller force they could bring to bear elsewhere.

"On another occasion we managed to salvage some hand grenades. We spent the next two or three weeks using them to booby-trap an area that contained aviation fuel bunkers. It was heavily guarded, so we had to be clandestine in our activities. When everything was in order, we fired .30 caliber tracer bullets to blow the tanks. Tracer bullets are so incendiary that they were glowing hot blue when they ignited the fuel tanks. The explosion was unbelievable! Then, as the Japanese ran for cover, they would trip the hand grenades. It was a scene of total mayhem.

"In November 1942, I led a group of fifteen Filipinos back into the Bataan Peninsula, where we found an abandoned ammunition dump that contained Lewis guns, .45 caliber handguns, and lots of ammunition. That find really helped us keep up our guerrilla activities.

"We always looked for hospitals when out on patrol, and this occasion we found a partly buried footlocker while rummaging near the ammunition dump. Inside we found four large bottles of sulfathiazole, an antibiotic, with 500 tablets in each. This was a spectacular find that would help Dr. Pineda save many a human life. The trunk also contained five metric quarts of medical alcohol. Someone had written on the bottles, 'To be consumed only by prescription of a doctor who is sober at the time.' We all thought that was pretty funny.

"Because there was such an abundance of supplies, we sent some of the men to get a pony to help us transport it back to camp. They also found some sweetened condensed milk, which was a real treat after the diet we'd been living on.

"By this time, the Japanese were apoplectic over our activities, and were trying to do anything possible to find and destroy us. They sent out companies of eighty or ninety men to hunt us down. Fortunately, it's almost impossible for even a large army to eradicate guerrillas in the jungle. We had the advantage of knowing the jungle, which provided deep, thick cover. What we couldn't control, however, was a lack of supplies. Eventually we ran out of ammunition, which put an end to our guerrilla warfare. With that, we found our way back to Fawcett's Camp.

"In May 1943, we'd been hiding out for more than a year. Call it good luck or a blessing, but so far, we'd been safe at Fawcett. Then one day, some of the local Filipinos approached us and said that they'd heard the Japanese were planning an attack on Fawcett. That gave us enough of a warning that we were able to slip out into the jungle. When the Japanese came, there were no foreigners there. The Japanese didn't believe the locals' excuses and threatened them with their lives if they found out they were lying.

"A few days later we returned back to camp to get some rice. They invited us to spend the night. I can still remember it today. There was a beautiful, star-filled sky. It felt good to be out of the jungle and back in the shelter of a small hut. After falling asleep, I thought I heard something out in the darkness. Suddenly, the Japanese started howling '*banzai!*' We almost jumped out of our skin, but their warning gave us just enough time to slip out of the hut and run to the jungle. As we ran through the cook's shack, I grabbed a bolo, which I was able to wrap around a Japanese soldier's neck as he was bearing down on us. I don't know how, but I managed to escape with my good friend Lou Barella, who was an Italian American from New Jersey.

"I don't know what reprisals the Japanese took against our hosts, but it was probably terrible. The Filipinos were the most freedom-loving people I have ever known. They knew what freedom was worth, and they were willing to risk everything for it. All of us held the Filipino people in the highest possible esteem. Quite simply, they saved our lives. In spite of all the threats by the Japanese and the various atrocities committed against the civilian population, the

Filipinos could always be trusted not to squeal on us. I came to love them with all my heart.

"I still don't know how they managed such effective communication in a time when they had no telephones, but the so-called 'bamboo telegraph' was very real and very effective. The Filipino people always seemed to know where the Japanese patrols were, and they passed the information through word of mouth, always managing to provide at least a half-hour notice before a patrol arrived at a particular location. That's how we managed to evade the Japanese as long as we did.

"After being ousted from Fawcett's Camp, we managed to live another two or three months in hiding. Finally, the Japanese found a way to drive us into a box canyon from which there was no escape. Their superior numbers, along with our lack of anything to use to fight back, gave them an overwhelming advantage. We had no choice but to surrender. My friends who had been with me from the beginning included Jack Finley, Lou Barella, and Colonel Magnuson. Our new guards took us to the San Fernando Provincial Prison.

"Life in prison was brutal and unforgiving. Because we had been living in the jungles for so long, it was automatically assumed that we were part of the guerrilla campaign, and that we had escaped from the death march. Either of those crimes was punishable by death. Of course, I was guilty on both counts, but I was wise enough to play dumb when the Japanese interrogators went after me. Despite the torture and beatings inflicted on me, I always maintained that I was just an ignorant soldier trying to find food and that I had no idea about Allied battle plans or an enforced march. No matter what they threw at me, I always held to that line. It was later that we learned that any prisoner who changed his story was summarily executed for having lied to them.

"As best as I can recollect, there were sixty-three Americans incarcerated in the San Fernando prison. All of us were soldiers who had previously escaped or who had never surrendered to the Japanese. Naturally, that made us prime victims of the Japanese, who hated us for our intransigence. Oh, the things they did to our men! One of the most horrifying was when they administered water torture to an American prisoner who was captured a few days after us. After strapping him to a board upside down, they forced a hose into his mouth and started pouring water in. Just when the prisoner was about to drown, they'd pull the hose out and start firing questions at him. When the prisoner didn't give the hoped-for responses, back in went the hose and they did it again. Unfortunately, in this one instance they went too far and the prisoner drowned right out on the parade field in front of us all. They simply cut his body loose and threw his corpse to the side for later burial. As outrageous as the water torture was, I have to admit that the first time this horrible form of brutality was used in the Philippines was by the Americans in the Spanish-American war in 1900–1902. By 1943, the Japanese had perfected it.

"One day, two of us managed to strike a small blow against our wardens. Some of our Filipino friends on the outside tossed a rope over the wall at a prearranged time, and we quickly pulled ourselves up and over the wall, where a one-horse cart was waiting for us on the other side. The local Filipinos who were helping us quickly covered us with kalabasa squash and whisked us out of town. We managed to avoid detection for nearly six weeks before being recaptured and returned to camp. We paid an awful price for those six weeks of freedom, but we accomplished the goal of harassing the Japanese.

"It was easy to lose track of time, with one day stretching forever into the next, but eventually we were transferred to Bilibid Prison in downtown Manila. Bilibid was an old colonial Spanish fort with three- to four-foot-thick walls, eighteen to twenty feet high. In the center of the compound, the Japanese prominently displayed an electric chair. During the hottest part of the day they made us stand out in the sun within eyesight of the chair just to intimidate us. We had to stand as close as possible to each other for hours on end, with no water, no food, and no shelter from the sun. On any given day, about a third of the prisoners fainted and dropped to the ground. Then the guards would kick and punch them to rouse them back into a standing position. When a prisoner could no longer get up, he was left to lie in the sun while the rest of us tried to avoid the beatings by remaining standing. I doubt any prisoner ever made it without falling at least a few times, but those of us in better physical condition were able to stand longer than most.

"At first, I was infuriated by this treatment, but after the guards broke down our physical reserves from lack of food and water, I didn't have the energy to hate them. I just prayed for nightfall so our ordeal could come to an end for another day. When it did, the guards would muster us out of formation and allow us to hobble over to the small huts where we were crowded in like sardines.

"By this time, most of us hated General MacArthur and all his officers. After all, they were the ones who had abandoned us to live in this misery. It just didn't make sense that with all the warnings about an impending invasion by the Japanese, they hadn't had an escape plan in place for all of the soldiers. The Philippines were our main naval base in the South Pacific, so we should have been better prepared. But we were the ones who had to pay the price for their lack of preparation. Believe me, the price was very high indeed. At first, I think everyone nurtured the hope that one day the Americans would return to help us, just like MacArthur had promised, but as the days and weeks wore on, we gave up the useless task of hoping and concentrated on simply surviving.

"For the next two and a half months, my companions and I endured the most creative torture imaginable. The guards were always trying to get secrets out of us that we simply didn't have. They seemed to delight in finding new ways to make our lives miserable. The interesting thing is, that as awful as torture was to endure personally, it was almost worse to hear the screams of other prisoners. The sounds of their agony grated against our ears and filled us with rage at our tormentors, leaving us with nothing but despair at our own impotence. It's amazing how the mind and spirit can hurt even more than the body.

"It's difficult, even now, to bring some of the things I witnessed to mind. The worst torture of all happened one day when I watched the guards pour battery acid into a man's eyes. They made all of us watch. The horror of the spectacle goes beyond words. As the man lay there writhing in pain, the guards did nothing to ease his pain. They wouldn't let any of us pour water in his eyes or do anything to comfort him. After enduring twenty minutes of unspeakable agony, he died of a heart attack. Other favored forms of torture were to insert bamboo shoots under a prisoner's fingernails or to beat a person's genitals with a bamboo cane on a table. The guards killed more than one female nurse with a broomstick. In short, they imposed any cruelty that their minds could conceive. Absolutely nothing was out of bounds. It goes without saying that ordinary beatings were part of virtually every interaction we had with these guards.

"I suppose a relevant question is: What rules helped some of us stay alive? First, stick to your story and never change it. Second, don't act weak, since it seemed like the guards homed in on the most vulnerable and attacked them with the greatest ferocity. On the other hand, you didn't want to act too cocky, or you'd be beaten down. Third, no matter what the guards said to you, you needed to do *something*, even if you didn't understand. They hated it when a prisoner seemed to ignore them. Fourth, use your ingenuity to get more food. Cigarettes were the universal medium of exchange, and by being a little innovative you could secure a small advantage. Finally, stick together. I think it really helped that I had friends that

I could talk to and encourage when they were down. Likewise, my friends helped me out when I got in trouble or depressed. It really came down to attitude. I decided that I was going to be a survivor, no matter what was thrown at me. I saw many men struggle and fight only to give up in the end. Whether from anger or stubbornness, I don't know, I was determined that I would make it. I think that's why I'm alive today to tell this story.

"Just how bad was it at Bilibid? I think the numbers speak for themselves. Of the sixty-three Americans I knew who had initially escaped the Death March and fought as guerrillas and who were subsequently captured, only seventeen lived to be transferred out. That's an astonishing mortality rate that speaks to the inhumanity that cost so many of my comrades their lives.

"When we shipped out to Cabanatuan in a narrow-gauge cattle car, we had to wear special red tags on our belts that indicated we were particularly dangerous. It was also a signal for guards up and down the line to slap us around a lot. After everything that had gone wrong up to this time, I was surprised, then, to find that our red tags actually gave us a break once we reached the new camp. Because we were considered dangerous and likely to escape, the camp commander gave orders forbidding us to go out on work detail, so we spent our time there working in the kitchen, cleaning toilets, and doing other odd jobs around the camp. That was a lot better than going out into the jungle with the other prisoners.

"Eventually we were transferred to Manila on a large troop transport ship. The conditions onboard were appalling, with more than 700 prisoners from all over the Philippines crowded down in the dark, dank hold of the ship. To accommodate the prisoners, the Japanese had built two tiers of bamboo platforms that we could sit on. It was so crowded, however, that only one-third could sit at a time, while the others had to stand. My good friend Jack Finley was claustrophobic, and after just a few minutes in this metal cellar, he started hyperventilating. I carried him back on top, with Paul Vacher helping the last few feet. Fortunately, the Japanese let him stay there long enough to catch his breath.

"Jack's experience was not unique; dozens of men fainted from the heat and overcrowding down in the hold. Finally, the Japanese were kind enough to open two more holds, which at least gave us enough room to sit down with our backs against each other. That made it a lot easier to sleep and to give our scrawny legs some relief.

"Probably the worst thing about being a prisoner is the overpowering boredom you have to deal with. There was just nothing to do except to sit around and talk and complain about conditions. The one thing we could do to relieve the tedium was to run a poker game. My connections with the Filipino underground made it so that I had a source for American money, which we used in the game. It also allowed us to buy off some of the guards, but that was a dangerous game to play. Paying cash was risky because the guards' officers might spot them using it to buy favors from other prisoners. Using cigarettes to do it was no problem, though, because everybody loved the popular form of currency, including the Japanese.

"Once the ship got under way, four of us who had formed a mutual support network while in Bilibid Prison got together again to help each other. These friends were Bill Main, Paul Vacher, and Millard Hileman. One was assigned to the laundry, which allowed him to keep us supplied with good soap, while another was assigned to the kitchen, allowing him to give us an extra ration of rice. I ran the poker game to bring in revenue. Of course, the only thing we could do with the money was to gamble or trade for food or other small items, which taught us a firsthand lesson in inflation. For example, I often paid $100 for a single pack of cigarettes—in 1940 dollars. On one occasion a sick man offered to pay another prisoner $20,000 for a bowl of rice, but the fellow just laughed at him. When I left the Philippines, I carried a bag with $76,000 in it. That's how much currency was in circulation with no place to go.

"I don't know how many Americans out of the 700 who were loaded onto the ship managed to survive the voyage. No records were kept. I do know that whenever a man died, his body was unceremoniously thrown overboard.

"A few weeks after setting sail, our captors allowed us to go on deck where they hosed everyone down. Water was a refreshing relief after spending weeks in the stinking hold of the ship. It felt wonderful to finally be clean. While I was savoring the experience of being hosed down, I noticed that the guard who was operating the hose turned suddenly to look out to sea. He let out a frantic shout and started gesturing wildly toward the side of the ship. He'd seen the trail of an American torpedo heading straight for the ship! We were under attack from an enemy submarine—at least it was an enemy to the Japanese. Of course, the submariners had no way of knowing that they were firing at American prisoners of war. Unfortunately, their aim was perfect, and a torpedo hit our ship full broadside. The effect of the explosion knocked me off my feet and left everyone on board dazed. The ship went down in what seemed a matter of minutes, and suddenly we found ourselves fighting our way frantically to the surface. Amazingly, a significant number of prisoners lived through the attack and managed to bob to the surface of the water, where we waited nervously until Japanese torpedo boats came and rescued us. There was no rest for the wicked, however, and in no time they simply transferred us to another ship, which proceeded without further incident to Formosa, on our way to Japan.

"It took us a month to complete the voyage from the Philippines to the island of Formosa (modern-day Taiwan). The caravan that our ship traveled in was very slow. Fortunately, I didn't suffer too much from seasickness, but it was still really miserable down in the hold if the waves were rough. The men who did have trouble with the motion made the decks slippery with their vomit, and a constant stench filled the air during the entire voyage.

"When we finally arrived in Formosa, the guards allowed the men to disembark from the ship for a few minutes on land, which felt great. After being at sea, my legs were unsteady and I swayed even though the ground was stable. Still, it was wonderful to breathe the air on land. Unfortunately, we counted only 500 prisoners who came off the ship, which meant that approximately 200 had died on the voyage up to that point.

"The ship pressed on to Japan. Once on land, my group was assigned to Fukuoka Camp No. 3, on the southern island of Kyushu, where we were transformed into slave laborers. There was no concern about us escaping here, because the entire population was Japanese and would happily turn us in if we got away from camp.

"The area supported a huge complex of steel mills, a large harbor, and a naval base that was located in this area to be close to the coal mines. The authorities divided the surviving American prisoners into three groups to work in each of these areas: steel work, coal mining, and harbor support for the navy. The work was very difficult, particularly since we were weak from malnourishment, lack of exercise, and the beatings we'd endured at the hands of the guards in the Philippines. The attitude we first encountered in Bataan was just as noticeable here, even though we were imprisoned by civilian guards. The Japanese simply could not believe that healthy men would ever surrender, and so they treated us with contempt. It did no good to explain that our officers had ordered us to surrender, or that we had actually fought a guerrilla campaign until we ran out of ammunition, so we just had to submit to their constant harassment and belittling. It was humiliating, and we were ashamed that we had been put into this position.

"In January of 1945, my friends and I were assigned to the Omine coal mines, where we worked 300 feet below the surface.

The work was extremely difficult and hazardous, particularly since there was poor ventilation and inadequate lighting in the mines. We were all scared that something bad would happen and, sure enough, one day our fears were confirmed when a large cave-in trapped us for three days in the darkness. That's as close as I ever came to thinking I would die, abandoned in a coal mine a million miles from home. Jumping ahead a bit in the story to emphasize just how bad the working conditions were: at the end of the war, only eleven of the more than four hundred prisoners in our group who made it to Japan still survived!

"We had no contact with the outside world while living in our little slave community. I'd learned to speak tolerable Japanese to communicate with the guards, but they couldn't provide any kind of information about how the war was going. They were always told that their troops were achieving great victories, and that the Allies were on the run all across the Pacific. Then, one day, everything turned upside down for our captors when a group of American B-29 bombers attacked in early March of 1945. That meant we were at risk as well because bombs don't distinguish between friend and foe. Still, it felt great to know that the Americans had established positions close enough to Japan that Allied bombers could strike the home islands. That had to mean that we were winning the war in the Pacific, and that meant there might actually be an end in sight. I doubt anything in the world could have bolstered our hopes more than the arrival of those bombers!

"One bomber stands out in memory because he earned the nickname 'Lonesome Joe.' Every day for several weeks, a lone B-29 bomber flew over the steel mill without dropping any bombs. It arrived at exactly the same time every day. He was probably just taking photographs, but his visit became a reason for us to silently celebrate. A few weeks later, a cloud of aircraft appeared in the skies and everyone hit the ground when American dive bombers screamed down to attack the steel factory powerhouse. One of the bombs blew up a ship filled with soybeans, and the explosion scattered soybeans for more than half a mile. The attack was very well planned, and it appeared that every bomber had a different target. Three or four minutes after the dive bombers' attack, a wing of B-17 bombers came in high and rained bombs on all available military targets. During the last six weeks of the war, they bombed us every single day at 1:00 P.M. I can easily understand the terror of the Japanese civilians because we were scared as well. There was nowhere to run or to hide; the bombs were so powerful that they could destroy anything they fell on. And while the bombing was amazingly accurate, a difference of just a few feet here or a few feet there meant the difference between life and death.

"On the day that World War II ended, my friends and I were busy at work. The entire island had been wired for a public-address system. Suddenly, a very emotional voice came on the speaker. All the Japanese froze in their tracks and looked to the east. It was the voice of the emperor. He declared that there was no defense against the atomic bomb and that the Japanese should not resist when the Americans arrived; they should simply go home. What an electrifying moment! The effect would have been almost comical if it had not created so much havoc. Once the Japanese heard their emperor instruct them to go home, they simply dropped their tools where they stood and walked away from the job to go home. In order to maintain control over the civilian population, the government had not allowed any Japanese citizens working in the war industry to serve in their hometown. So now everyone was anxious to return to their homes.

"Even the engineers on a prisoner transport train just abandoned the locomotive right where it was when the announcement came. Eventually, some of the Americans climbed into the cab of the train and brought the prisoners back to camp. After the guards abandoned us, we spread out to get food and take whatever we could find. All transportation froze, and in the first week after the announcement, Japan was totally shut down. There was no power where we lived.

"We encountered an amazing incident on the third day after the war ended. Three B-17 bombers circled overhead. I was standing next to a chaplain that had been taken prisoner and who had become a good friend. When the bomb-bay doors opened, he let out a curse and said that the crew probably didn't realize the war was over! Wouldn't that be something, to be killed by American bombs three days after the war ended? But instead of bombs, food started raining down! What a miracle, and what a tribute to America! Just days after the war had ended, they were taking action to feed their former enemies. We were so grateful to get food and we were so proud of our country.

"None of us had tasted meat in well over a year. There were a number of Sikhs from India who had been imprisoned with us and when they saw the food packages land on the other side of a masonry wall, they broke down the wall to get to the food. Among the items of food available were cans of corned beef. Someone said to eat just one can, and most of the men did stop eating once they were full. But three of the Sikhs just kept eating and eating because they had been so starved. It was an unfortunate mistake, because they got so sick from putting rich food in their stomachs after the meager diet that we had been living on, that they doubled over in pain. Eventually, all three died.

"Sometime before the end of the war, seven of us had witnessed the huge mushroom cloud created by the explosion of the atomic bomb over Hiroshima. After the war ended we wanted to see what had happened, so we went to the shore and found a barge to take us over to what had been a submarine base near Hiroshima. What an incredible, awful sight! Only a few buildings that had been constructed of concrete were left partially standing. In some places, you could see where a shadow had fallen on the wall, leaving an impression that wasn't as badly burned. Other than these few remnants, everything had been reduced to rubble. The citizens of Hiroshima had no idea what had hit them—they had simply been atomized the instant the bomb exploded. We later learned that people who lived further out of the city and that had been looking in the direction of the bomb when it exploded had their eyes melted in the sockets. As we stood in the powder of what had been a great city, the man next to me started weeping.

"As long as I live I'll never forget the horrifying sights that greeted us in the aftermath of the atomic bomb. Anything within a mile of ground zero was completely destroyed—there were no human or animal remains to be seen. The ground under our feet was still hot, and there was no ash—just an incredibly fine powder. Beyond one mile we discovered parts of charred bodies. Further out the inhabitants survived, but they were in horrible physical condition.

"One of the biggest problems associated with the bomb is that three rivers run through Hiroshima. When the bomb exploded, all the water in the rivers vaporized. This caused a tidal wave of water coming in from the ocean to fill the void. Some of the people who had survived the blast of the bomb were killed by the tidal wave.

"Many thousands of people were killed, not by the blast of the bomb, but by suffocation because the heat of the bomb consumed all available oxygen. Many miles away, the trees that remained standing all pointed to Hiroshima, having been bent inward by the huge vacuum created by the explosion.

"As the occupation army arrived in greater numbers, they came and liberated us. It felt so great to go into a big tent where they allowed us to shower and deloused us. They gave us new clothing, although none of it fit properly, but who cared about that! Later we were given uniforms in the correct size.

"On April 25, 1945, they took us out through Nagasaki Harbor. This great harbor sits between two mountain ranges, and we could see how the concussion of the bomb went up both sides of the mountain ranges. Before the war, Nagasaki had a large and prominent skyline, but now everything was destroyed. We could see where the railroad tracks had melted and the ties turned into white powder.

"The prisoners in the worst medical condition went to the hospital ship. I was transferred to an aircraft carrier, which went to Okinawa. I then went by cruiser to the Philippines. When we arrived back in the Philippines, we naturally wanted to find our Filipino friends but were told we would have no leave of absence. Four of us quickly solved that problem by hijacking a military police jeep. We spent the next six weeks out in the provinces visiting friends and revisiting the places where we had spent so much of the war in hiding.

"Finally, we went back to Manila. The provost arrested us and put us in jail. After the fifth day of confinement, I guess he felt guilty for incarcerating former prisoners of war, so he told us that we could go free, but had to find our own way home. We went down to Nichols Field, which had been completely rebuilt. We sat around a command post for two or three hours. Then I saw a lieutenant colonel that I thought I recognized, so I turned to him and said, 'Do I know you?' It turned out that his name was Colonel Forinash, and I had known him when he was a lieutenant. He was happy to see that I was still alive, even though I looked terrible. After catching up on what had happened to each other, he helped us gain passage on a C-52 cargo plane and then pulled strings to get us through to Guam. We took a plane to Hawaii. I spent several days there enjoying the sun, then found an aircraft with just one seat left and happily found that all the others were occupied by nurses. Not bad after four years in the jungle and as a prisoner of war!

"Arriving in San Francisco, I was assigned to the Presidio. Shortly thereafter, I was transferred to the Camp Carson hospital near Colorado Springs, Colorado, to recuperate from my war injuries and illnesses. After three months, I got to go home for a few days, and then back to Colorado for another three and a half months in the hospital. Finally, I went to Denver, where I was discharged from the service on March 1, 1946.

"After getting my health back a bit, I went to two years of college in Southern California to study journalism and then transferred to Columbia, Missouri. I was an honor student in both agriculture and journalism. Then I got a job at a newspaper in Muskogee, Oklahoma. From there, I went to work for a radio station in Freeport, Illinois. Eventually I went to work for the agricultural corporation Cargill, where I spent twenty years in the livestock feed division as a sales training manager and sales manager.

"In the years since World War II, every one of the former prisoners of war I stayed in contact with suffered from post-traumatic stress disorder and at some point or another went totally out of control. I suffered just like the rest, but eventually managed to find peace. When my family joined a new church, I found a new perspective on the world, and a new way of dealing with the memories that remained. It also helped that through the years I was active in veterans' associations and kept in touch with many of the other survivors of the Bataan campaign and Japanese imprisonment. Having friends who were there made it easier to keep my sanity.

"Now that it is far past, I can tell you that I am so proud to have served with the men and women who defended the Philippines. Had it not been for our efforts, Japan may have occupied Australia, which could have had a profound impact on the ultimate course of the war. Certainly, our efforts prevented immense suffering. That was just one of the benefits of our ordeal. The men I served with are among the best I have ever known, and I hope that this brief record will properly honor the sacrifices that they made so many years ago. Out of approximately 22,000 Americans captured in the Philippines, only 15,000 returned home—a death rate of more than 30 percent. By comparison, only 3 percent of Americans captured in Europe perished. Ours was a unique experience. To me, the men with whom I shared this ordeal are among the greatest heroes in our nation's history."

AFTERWORD

Pat Patton passed away on March 16, 2007. He received the Bronze Star and was an honoree at the World War II Memorial dedication ceremony in Washington, DC, in 2004.

CHAPTER 2

NANCY WAKE

THE WHITE MOUSE OF
THE FRENCH RESISTANCE

I too believed in freedom. I was young but I already knew the horrors a totalitarian state could bring, and long before the Second World War was declared, I also understood that a free world can only remain free by defending itself against any form of aggression. I knew too that freedom itself could not be permanent. It has to be defended at all costs, even if by doing so part of our freedom has to be sacrificed. It will always be in danger because, alas, victory is not permanent."[1]

The Nazi soldiers who publicly tormented Jews in a town square in Vienna in the pre-war days of 1938 were unaware that a young woman watching from the sidelines would end up saving the lives of hundreds of other Jews and thousands of Allied military servicemen while also contributing to the deaths of thousands of their Nazi foes once war broke out. Their inhuman cruelty so outraged the young Australian woman that she would soon risk everything to help destroy the Third Reich and those who fought on its behalf. That woman, Nancy Grace Augusta Wake, said later, "People have often asked me how I came to work against the Germans. It was easy. It was in Vienna that I resolved that if I ever had the chance, I would do anything, however big or small, stupid or dangerous, to try and make things more difficult for their rotten party. More than hatred or anger, I felt a deep loathing for the Nazis."[2]

This was no idle resolve—in time she delivered difficulties to the Nazi war effort beyond imagination. In the beginning of the war, Nancy Wake helped hundreds of Allied soldiers and frightened Jews escape from southern France to neutral Spain by accompanying them on train rides to the frontier, often under the very noses of officials who were looking for her. So effective was her leadership in this underground railroad that she was soon dubbed the "White Mouse" by the Gestapo for her remarkable ability to escape detection. She eluded capture even with a reward of 500,000 francs on her head, ultimately making the tortuous crossing of the Pyrenees mountain range into Spain.

Later in the war she gave up this hard-won freedom to parachute back into northern France, where she was instrumental in setting up communication and supply lines to support 7,000 *maquisards* (rural French Resistance fighters) who successfully tied down 22,000 German soldiers, along with 1,000 trucks and ten military aircraft.[3] Her *maquisards* also conducted a targeted campaign of sabotage to prepare for the expected Allied landings in France on D-Day in 1944. With Nancy's help and leadership they blew up bridges, destroyed vital rail links that the Germans depended on for resupply and troop movements, and stole foodstuffs and war matériel from German convoys. This harassment of the Germans sapped their morale while leaving them dangerously exposed to Allied assaults. And at the heart of it all was Nancy Wake, who used radio communications with England to arrange parachute drops of explosives and ammunition to more than ten secret landing zones from which they were distributed to Resistance fighters.

Consider one example that illustrates her courage and resolve: After distributing airlifted ammunition to Resistance fighters in an active zone, Nancy's car was attacked by a German aircraft. She barely escaped death, diving from the car just moments before it was blown up. Fearful that they would be captured, Nancy's radio operator destroyed his radio and codes so they would not fall into German hands. This left the *maquisards* in her district with no means of communication to coordinate future air drops with London.

So Nancy volunteered to ride a bicycle more than 150 miles (250 kilometers) through German-occupied lines to ask another radio operator in a different zone to request a new radio and code book for Nancy's area. Everyone thought it was crazy for a single woman to travel alone through occupied France, but she argued that it was precisely because she was an attractive woman that she would get through. A single man riding through the countryside would almost certainly be identified as a *maquisard* and shot on the spot, but she felt that a woman would raise less suspicion.

Finally, after much discussion, they allowed her to go. Riding as fast as possible, Nancy always slowed a bit when approaching a group of German soldiers to make it appear she was out cycling for leisure. She carried a turnip or carrot to suggest she'd been to the market. Most of the time she got by with just a wave and a smile, but, when forced to pass through a German checkpoint, she innocently asked if the German sentries needed to search her. It was fortunate that she spoke perfect French from her pre-war life as the socialite wife of a wealthy industrialist in Marseille. Not once was she challenged, and she managed to make the contact and request the new radio equipment. When she returned from her three-hundred-mile roundtrip a few days later, her legs were literally raw from chafing and she was unable to sit or walk for days. Yet in spite of the excruciating pain, she forged ahead and secured the new radio when it was dropped at a prearranged spot. Because of her courage and fortitude, the Resistance was back in business.[4]

By the end of the war, Nancy Wake was the most highly decorated Australian in World War II. Her awards and medals included the Companion of the Order of Australia, the George Medal from England, the Officier de Légion d'Honneur and Croix de Guerre (three times) from France, the Medal of Freedom (with Bronze Palm) from the United States, and the Returned and Services' Association (RSA) Badge in Gold from New Zealand, where she was born in 1912. The French, New Zealand, and Australian awards are the highest distinctions given by those governments, while the George Medal and Medal of Freedom are the second-highest distinctions awarded to civilians by England and the United States.

Nancy Wake's service in the cause of freedom was remarkable; her unique and fearless personality allowed her to take risks unimaginable to most people. But her courage came at a heavy price as she placed those she loved in harm's way.

A DAUGHTER OF NEW ZEALAND, AUSTRALIA, ENGLAND, AND FRANCE

Nancy was born in Wellington, New Zealand, on August 30, 1912. Her family moved to North Sydney, Australia, in 1914, but her father quickly returned to New Zealand, leaving his wife to raise their six children as a single parent. Nancy was both a capable and a restless girl. It fell to her to cook for her family, and often to clean the house. She didn't like these household chores at all and made multiple attempts to run away from home. At the age of sixteen, she was successful in breaking with her family and soon found work as a nurse in what was then called a lunatic asylum. The inmates loved her.

When she inherited a small sum of money from an aunt, she decided to see the world, traveling first to New York City and then to London. From that point, she was on her own. In England she became a journalist, eventually working as a European correspondent for the Hearst newspapers out of Paris. She loved the French people and quickly adapted to both their language and their culture. Nancy had a natural gift for *savoir-faire* (the ability to speak appropriately in all social settings) and could act with a cheeky grace that delighted her French friends. What had been considered stubborn restlessness in Australia was viewed as witty and urbane in France, and she finally felt at home. It was during her travels throughout Europe in the 1930s that she witnessed the brutish behavior of the Nazis toward the Jews, particularly in Austria after the German *Anschluss*, which effectively annexed Austria in 1938. On more than one occasion she saw "roving Nazi gangs randomly beating Jewish men and women in the streets."[5]

In early 1939, Nancy was introduced to Henri Fiocca while visiting Cannes in southern France. Her beautiful good looks attracted Fiocca, one of the wealthiest men in Marseille, even though Nancy was just twenty-three years old. He was thirty-seven. Fiocca always seemed to have beautiful women with him, which raised Nancy's curiosity. She didn't understand why he never approached her. When she confronted him about how he secured dates with such a variety of attractive ladies, he replied, "They call me." She was incredulous that they would initiate the contact. "Yes," he replied, "every girl but the one I want rings me up." The light went on for Nancy, who quickly replied, "If you want to speak with me, Fiocca, you will ring me up!"[6] He did call her, and soon they fell in love. Although his family was opposed, he proposed marriage to the impetuous young Australian and she accepted.

With money and prestige as Fiocca's fiancée, Nancy found her world much expanded. The housework she so despised in Australia now fell to hired servants. Fiocca was a genial man who indulged Nancy while introducing her to the most prominent people in the area. Her quick wit and audacious behavior delighted her fiancé, and he enjoyed bringing her into his world of casinos and expensive dinners, parties, and receptions. In spite of her humble beginnings in life, she quickly adapted yet again to fit into this new role.

With her marriage set for November 1939, she decided to make one last trip to England to visit old friends. Arriving there in August, she was in England when the Nazis invaded Poland in September. War broke out within days and, even though she longed to return to France, she felt it her duty to volunteer to help England in the fight. After all, Australia was still part of the English Commonwealth, even though it had been politically independent since 1901. All the English could offer her for work was in a NAAFI (Navy, Army and Air Force Institutes) facility to run recreational facilities and sell goods to servicemen and their families. This was not at all appealing to Nancy, who had envisioned more of a combat role, and so she went through the difficult process of finding passage back to Cannes. She and Henri Fiocca were married on November 30, 1939.

For the next few months Nancy lived an extravagant lifestyle, buying expensive dresses, going with Henri to tony restaurants, all the while knowing that he would soon be called up to serve in the French military. But Nancy was not entirely frivolous. As the time for Henri's summons to military duty drew closer, she insisted that she wanted to go to the front as well. This astounded her husband, who asked what she would do. "Drive an ambulance," she replied. When he told her that there were no ambulances available, she insisted that he convert one of his company's trucks into an ambulance so she could take it to the front. He thought it a joke, so he promised he would have her trained and equipped. When he was drafted, Nancy held him to this promise and soon she made her way to northern France where the war was taking place. It was there that she saw the horrors of war firsthand.

She used her ambulance to evacuate wounded soldiers as well as refugees. When winter came, the roads became nightmares of mud and blood, and Nancy was in the thick of it. She drove past police guards to reach the very edge of the front lines, where she picked up anyone who needed help, including Belgian refugees who were fleeing their homes in terror. The fighting was horrific, and Nancy forced herself to continue, in spite of her revulsion to blood and death. When it became obvious that Belgium would soon fall to the Germans, she retreated back to Paris, taking as many people with her as possible. She was in Paris when France capitulated to the Nazis on June 13, 1940. Along with most French citizens, she felt humiliated for her adopted country and desolate at the thought of German dominance over France. Realizing that she did not want to stay in the occupied part of France, she took her ambulance south toward Marseille. After it gave out because of mechanical problems, Nancy walked the balance of the way back home. She was grateful to find that Henri had also made it home safely.

The Fioccas now entered a new phase of life. Marseille was in the unoccupied territory known as Vichy France. Germany did not officially rule here, but the government headquartered in the small city of Vichy was sympathetic to Germany and hostile to England. Vichy agreed to aid the German war effort with food and non-resistance so the Germans could concentrate their military forces elsewhere. In return, the Germans left the southern half of France out of the fighting and under the control of the French government. Nancy and Henri hated this—to see the Germans advancing through Europe and at war with England, while in their beautiful city of Marseille, life went on undisturbed. Of course, there was rationing of food, gasoline, and other commodities needed by the Germans, but the Fioccas managed to buy what they needed on the black market. Soon, they had settled into a comfortable routine in which the Blitz in London with its fire and destruction seemed like a fantasy, something they despised but could do nothing about. It was both discouraging and easy.

That changed one day when a chance encounter at a local bar connected Nancy and Henri to a young Englishman who had been interned at the local fortress when war broke out. He was essentially a prisoner of war, but one with a parole to go into the city of Marseille as long as he made no attempt to escape. Like the Fioccas, he was frustrated to know that his country was under attack while he lounged in relative comfort on the French Riviera. Nancy invited him, along with two friends, to dinner. She used her skill in the black market to buy extra food. During dinner with her three guests and Henri, the Englishmen pointed out that there were more than 200 officers at the fortress who wanted to escape. Of course they could not do that while on parole into the city, since that would both violate their honor and end their freedom to move about. But they knew that there were other ways to escape from their prison. The only problem was how to get from deep inside France to a neutral country where they could repatriate to England. If someone could help them find their way to the Spanish border, they could cross the Pyrenees to the south and then make their way back to England.

Henri knew that this was just the sort of thing Nancy would embrace. To her it was a matter of duty. But for him, it would place everything at risk—if he assisted Nancy in helping British soldiers to escape, he would place his extended family in jeopardy if she was discovered. His entire fortune would be lost, his factory seized, and even his life forfeited if he were found to be aiding and abetting the enemy. Nancy talked with him about it, and Henri agreed to help. Thus was born Nancy's first life as a member of the French Resistance.

It started out small. Nancy and Henri welcomed four or five Englishmen per day into their flat. This was not viewed as suspect by the local police, since everyone knew that Nancy was British by birth, and the men who came were on parole. But then one day, Captain Ian Garrow arrived as part of the group. A Scotsman of great cunning, he was not on parole, but had escaped from the fortress and was the subject of a manhunt. While in hiding he had connected with sympathetic French and Spanish guides near the Spanish border who wished to do the Germans harm by helping escaped Allied soldiers as well as endangered citizens (mostly Jewish refugees) find their way into Spain. He asked for Nancy's help in setting up an underground railroad by acting as both a messenger and an escort. Nancy agreed, as Henri knew she would. While he did not openly provide any assistance—to do so would have imperiled everyone—Henri provided substantial financial support whenever Nancy asked for money.

In the beginning, Nancy started carrying documents to and from Cannes. Then she mentioned her plight to a French friend known as Commander Busch, who had come south from occupied France. He had shown his anti-Nazi leanings early. When Nancy mentioned she was going to Cannes, he asked if she would drop off some radio equipment to a "man" in Lyon. She agreed, and even offered the Resistance free use of a retreat Henri owned in Névache. This soon became an important resting point on the underground railroad. In time, Nancy was making frequent runs to Cannes, Lyon, Toulouse, and Nice. She was able to do this because she was Madame Fiocca of Marseille, traveling with legitimate French papers. In addition to acting as a courier, she also often accompanied escaping prisoners and refugees to given them legitimacy while traveling on French railroads. In little time, the number of people she assisted numbered in the hundreds—a detail that was not lost on the French authorities and the Nazis who had outposts in southern France. Although officially unoccupied, the Riviera was allowed as a rest and relaxation spot for German military, and so the Gestapo had officers there to monitor German interests.

It wasn't long before the Resistance operations were noticed by both the Germans and the French. The Vichy French were anxious to shut it down so that Germany did not move in to occupy this part of France. The Germans were anxious to shut it down to prevent the escape of British and other prisoners who could return to active duty to fight against Germany. And Nancy's success was definitely noticed, although no one could identify her as the mysterious woman who was known to be aiding the effort. Thus, she earned the code name "White Mouse" by the Gestapo and local Vichy officials. Apparently, a white mouse is very hard to detect and catch, even though it operates out in the open. So it was with Nancy.

In time, she started helping American aviators who were shot down fighting the Nazis. To do this, she traveled under false identities. She did not want to put her status as Henri Fiocca's wife in jeopardy by using her real name on the many and frequent train trips she was now taking through the French countryside. In addition, she continued to help escaping Jews and other non-military citizens who were in trouble with the Vichy authorities. It was a massive operation that was attracting increasing scrutiny by the Gestapo. Nancy's risk increased with every trip.

Finally, the Gestapo started to close in. They tapped the Fioccas' phone lines, and a friendly bartender told Nancy that Gestapo agents had been watching her. There was a price of 500,000 francs being offered for information leading to the arrest of the White Mouse, which meant that ordinary citizens were watching everywhere for clues as to who this person might be. Henri insisted that his wife escape to Spain, promising that he would soon follow. It took Nancy many attempts to make it across the border. She was actually arrested twice while using a false identity and was very close to being exposed when one of the local members of the Resistance appeared at her jail cell to claim her as his mistress. He said that she was traveling outside of Marseille because she was afraid of her husband's jealousy. Incredible as it seems, this excuse seemed justified to the French jailers since such a thing was not unusual. They let her go.

On another occasion, she was on a train toward the border with Spain when the train started to slow unexpectedly. Word came that the Germans had set up an ambush to capture her. To evade this, Nancy leaped from the window of the moving train and made her way to an emergency rendezvous spot where she once again disappeared into the crowd. Finally, after many aborted attempts, she made it to the border. All that stood between her and safety were the Pyrenees, and in the dead of winter she and a small group started the tortuous climb to the high mountain passes. Here is one of her biographers describing part of Nancy's experience:

> On the second part of their forty-seven hour trek they were lashed with a biting snowstorm. A blizzard raged and the ice and snow cut into them like needles. But they pressed on through it. One of the Americans cried out that they must halt, he could go no farther. Nancy slapped him savagely and he went on. One of the girls said she could go no farther. Nancy whispered to Jean, and Jean calmly tripped the girl into an icy stream. Then she had to go on or freeze to death.
>
> But finally it ended. They reached a hut, lit a fire, dried their clothes and waited till nightfall. Ahead lay a river. When they crossed that river they were out of German-controlled Europe and into Spain. Nancy slept badly as she waited on this last leg of her dash for

freedom. There were several alarms, but nothing came of them.

Then, under cover of darkness, they eluded the sentries, crossed the river and left the sentries behind them.

"Henri, my dear," Nancy muttered as she reached the other side, "I hope you'll be as lucky in your journey as I've been."[7]

Nancy Wake Fiocca soon had found freedom. Her husband was not so fortunate. Soon after her escape, Henri Fiocca was arrested, tortured, and executed for aiding and abetting the enemy. Nancy had a dream in England that woke her with a fright. Even though Henri was not in the dream, she interpreted it to mean that he had been killed. Her friends comforted her, telling her that it was nothing more than a dream; but in reality her fears were true, and she always blamed herself for putting her gentle and generous husband in harm's way.

AN AUSTRALIAN LEADER IN
THE FRENCH *MAQUIS*

After paying a Spanish official a handsome bribe, courtesy of Henri Fiocca's money, Nancy and the others in her group were turned over to the British consul and returned to England. For several weeks she slept as much as possible to recover from the rigors of her escape and prior service. When it became clear that Henri was not likely to escape to England anytime soon, her restless nature asserted itself and she volunteered to go back to France as a saboteur. She was accepted into the Special Order Executive (SOE) and underwent rigorous physical and psychological training in England and Scotland. Here she learned to make her way through bomb fields, obstacle courses, and how to fire a Bren gun (machine gun). She proved to be a crack shot. She also learned the very precise measurements required to make explosives out of everyday household chemicals that could be purchased in France. These were needed to supplement or substitute for military explosives parachuted in. Her good nature and keen sense of humor endeared her to the men in her training group and she soon earned their respect as well. With her flair for entertaining, she organized parties and entertainment when they had leave. In spite of the extreme physicality of the training, Nancy survived and soon parachuted into northern France to facilitate communication with London and to manage the finances of the *Maquis* (French Resistance) in her assigned area.

As noted earlier, her group was extremely successful. When Nancy first arrived in France, the locals knew her only as Madame Andrée. London identified her over the radio as Hélène. No one knew her real name. At first, the local French thought that they could gain access to the money and arms shipments she controlled without actually submitting to London's command. But Nancy was a shrewd character, secretly listening to their conversations (again, relying on her nearly perfect grasp of the French language). With one particularly troublesome Resistance leader, she learned that he intended to have one of his men seduce her, then murder her in the bed to steal her money. Nancy resisted his advances, saying that she had no intention of being killed or of fraternizing with this man. With this group, she withheld both money and arms, directing London's largess to other groups. Within a month, Nancy had taken complete control of the situation by making it clear that she would distribute matériel and money only when the local French submitted to her idea of military discipline. In doing so she became the de facto leader of nearly 7,500 men.

As the war progressed, Nancy's 7,500 Maquis killed more than 1,200 Germans at a loss of just 100 of their own number.[8] Plus, they created all sorts of confusion and mischief for the frustrated Nazis. This included cutting supposedly secret telephone lines buried by the Nazis and destroying a steel factory and a railroad junction. Her area in the mountainous area of Auvergne in Central France caused the most trouble of any for the Germans, who went to great lengths to find and destroy the Resistance.

Nancy showed both her courage and her resolve on many occasions. In one, she crept upon a German SS guard and used a karate chop to his throat to kill him before he could raise an alarm. His death was close to instantaneous. In another incident, she found that the men of the Maquis had been abusing a woman known to be a German spy. Rather than kill her immediately, they kept her alive but in horrible circumstances. Nancy interviewed the woman to confirm for herself that she was a spy. Then she ordered her immediate death to protect the safety of her unit and to prevent further suffering to the woman. Nancy knew very well that if she were ever captured, her sentence would be death, likely preceded by torture and abuse, and she was not going to inflict the latter on another person. She then interviewed two other women taken prisoner by some Maquis under her command and, upon determining that they were innocent, immediately set them free with a return of their money. One was so grateful that she stayed on as Nancy's assistant.

As the war closed in on the Germans, Nancy and her group moved against the Vichy regime, which most Frenchmen by this time considered traitorous to France for collaborating with the Nazis. The Resistance fighters were welcomed as heroes. When Nancy and her chief officers made their way to Marseille, she learned the terrible circumstances of Henri's death. A Nazi sympathizer had infiltrated the underground railroad and used his knowledge to betray Henri. He was tortured mercilessly. Twice he was offered freedom if only he would betray Nancy's whereabouts. His own father was used to make these offers, but Henri resolutely refused. His death was Nancy's only regret. She also discovered that the Nazis had confiscated all of their wealth, so she was no longer wealthy. In fact, she had to use her accumulated earnings to pay off the debts Henri had left behind.

After the war, Nancy Wake returned first to Paris, then to London, and finally to Sydney. There she twice tried to run for political office, both times nearly besting a seasoned member of Parliament, but ultimately failed. She married a second time. When her second husband, John Forward, died forty years after their marriage, she returned to London a final time. She passed away on August 7, 2011, at age ninety-eight.

Nancy Wake spoke the first words in this chapter, and she certainly deserves the last:

> You see, I was lucky. I was in France at the beginning, when the Germans were right on top. And I was still in France at the end when we saw the Germans on the run. I know how Frenchmen felt all that time. I'd been part of their existence for a long while. I love France—people just don't realize how much she suffered. Six hundred thousand French people died because of World War II: two hundred and forty thousand of them in prisons and concentration camps. And yet there were always escape routes and "safe houses" for our men shot down over there and trying to get away. There was always a Resistance movement.
>
> . . . I'm glad I was there. I'm glad I did what I did. I hate wars and violence but, if they come, then I don't see why we women should just wave our men a proud good-bye and then knit them balaclavas. . . . You see, in those days we knew what we were fighting and we had a job to do. We did it. I may have lost a lot during the war, 'specially Henri: but I made a lot of friends and I did what I felt I had to do.[9]

CHAPTER 3

JOSEPH HYALMAR ANDERSON
MISSING IN ACTION

Joseph Hyalmar Anderson enlisted in the United States Navy on November 20, 1942. Prior to the war, he went by his middle name, pronounced "Yalmer" by family and friends; but he went by Joe in the military. His Lockheed PV-1 Ventura Patrol Bomber went missing thirteen months later on December 26, 1943, while on a routine training patrol off Vancouver Island, British Columbia, Canada. Two days later, his parents received a telegram declaring their son officially Missing in Action (MIA). His mother broke down in sobs, her heart filled with a mixture of dread and hope. His father threw the telegram in the fireplace.

The anxiety felt by Hyalmar's family on learning of his disappearance was similar to that shared by more than 72,000 other World War II families whose sons or fathers went MIA.[1]

Missing in Action is a casualty classification given to a member of the military who cannot be located, having been killed, wounded, captured, or deserted from their active combat unit. For their loved ones, MIA status begins a tortured period of uncertainty where hope for the eventual return of the missing soldier erodes with each passing day that he or she does not show up. The best outcome is when an MIA soldier is simply separated from his or her main unit in the confusion of battle and is temporarily adopted by another group. Occasionally an MIA soldier is reclassified as a prisoner of war when the enemy notifies the International Red Cross. Most often, however, those designated as MIA have perished, and the location of their deaths are never known. Of all those who serve, the MIAs are truly invisible, with nothing but memories to honor their sacrifice. They are remembered by those at home, mostly in old photographs, childhood mementos, and by the military, who set up POW/MIA tables at most military functions.[2] No funerals, just memorial services, with no remains to bring closure.

J. HYALMAR ANDERSON

Hyalmar was born May 5, 1924, in the small farming community of Taylor, Utah, approximately five miles outside the railroad town of Ogden. He was born two years to the day after his older brother, Irvin. The boys were best friends, growing together in the years between the great wars of the twentieth century. He and Irvin worked hard on the farm and took any other job they could find when available, as money was hard to come by in the hardscrabble years of the Great Depression. Hyalmar had a natural talent for drawing that his sixth-grade teacher wanted to develop with art lessons, but the family couldn't afford such a luxury.

As teenagers, Irvin and Hyalmar took on the physically challenging task of stacking pea vines during the harvest. The automatic pea viner ran from fourteen to sixteen hours a day, automatically stripping the pods from the vines, then shelling the peas for canning. Mounds of pea vines had to be manually lifted from the machine and carried to an ever-growing stack, a dusty and heavy job. The Anderson boys did this work with no complaint.[3]

In November 1942, Hyalmar was just seventeen years old when his brother Irvin enlisted in the Navy. Hyalmar wanted to join as well, which required his father's permission. His father reluctantly signed the waiver so Hyalmar could enlist, and the two young men went off to Camp Farragut in northern Idaho for basic training. Hyalmar wrote in his service diary that "at that time my height was 6 ft., 140 lbs., brown eyed, red hair, light complexion, waist 34 inches, shirt size 15, shoe size 5E, socks 11 1/2, undershirt 34, and shorts 34."[4]

In other words, he was like most other young service members from a farm background: lean, muscular, and anxious to serve. From Farragut, he went to Oklahoma to train as a naval gunner. He then transferred to Seattle, Washington, as an Aviation Ordnanceman Third Class. His crew was training to go to the Solomon Islands in the South Pacific.

LOST IN HEAVY WEATHER

On Sunday, December 26, 1943, Lockheed PV-1 Ventura #28736 departed Whidbey Island on a routine navigation training flight under the command of pilot Lieutenant Joseph Robert Cranny of Grinnell, Iowa, with copilot Ensign Charles Schoenfelder of Wathena, Kansas. Other members of the crew included Robert Maguet (Portsmouth, Ohio), Joseph Winslow, Jr. (Pittsburgh, Pennsylvania), Ernest Morgan (Rockville, Virginia), and Hyalmar Anderson (Ogden, Utah). Lieutenant Cranny was an experienced pilot in the United States Naval Reserve. During the course of the flight, extremely bad weather developed, with rains recorded as heavy even for that part of Canada. Visibility dropped to near zero. The flight never returned to base. Some reports suggest that bad weather cancelled all flights in the area for the next ten days. After that, all searches for the missing aircraft proved futile. Demands of the war limited the availability of crews and aircraft, and the Navy abandoned the search.

It was six months later, in June 1943, that the fate of the lost aircraft finally revealed itself. During a routine scouting flight, a Canadian crew from Coal Harbour Military Air Base spotted an area of sheared-off pine trees at Lawn Point near Quatsino Sound. Moving in to take a closer look, they spotted the wreckage of the Ventura, which had obviously attempted an emergency landing in this unpopulated and geographically remote area of the island. They contacted the US Naval Air Station at Whidbey Island, Washington, with the tail numbers of the stricken aircraft. On June 16, representatives of the US Navy joined their counterparts from the Royal Canadian Air Force in Coal Harbour to make a trip by speedboat to the site of the crash.

There they were surprised to find evidence that crewmembers had survived the crash, including remnants of a well-used path from the beach leading up to the wreckage of the aircraft. The remains of a fire pit and fish bones indicated that meals had been prepared and eaten. A second path through the thick grass led down to a different spot on the beach where they discovered a remnant of the aircraft's plexiglass windshield propped against a rock in such a fashion that it would reflect the sun's rays in the direction of the small town of Winter Harbour. There was also a makeshift flagpole from which one of Hyalmar Anderson's T-shirts hung to attract attention.

Following the original path to the wreckage, the investigators found an angled row of logs placed tightly together. At the top of the angle was a log placed perpendicular to the others. Under these logs, investigators found the remains of five members of the crew, placed carefully side by side, a makeshift grave designed to protect the bodies from the elements and perhaps wild animals as much as possible. The investigators discovered that two of the crewmembers had suffered broken bones which had started to knit back together—proof that those men were alive for some period after the crash.

The only crewmember not accounted for was Joseph Hyalmar Anderson. It was clear that he had lived long enough to wear the two paths through the grass, as well as to watch each of his comrades perish from exposure and starvation. As tail gunner positioned at the back of the aircraft, it is possible that he suffered the fewest injuries, which is why he outlived the others. His flag and mirror clearly show that he hoped to attract attention and rescue; but no one had found him. For some unknown reason, perhaps because of the pressures of the war, the US Navy failed to notify the Royal Canadian Air Force or the villagers across the harbor that the Ventura was missing, so no one was looking for them. No one has yet found Hyalmar's remains.

It is possible that he decided to try to find his way to civilization—just five miles across the water, but much farther traveling overland because of the bay. Moreover, the topography of that part of Vancouver Island was steep to the point of being nearly impassable even in good weather with adequate food and clothing. During one of the most severe winters on record, he simply could not have survived such a journey. Even to this day, this theory is pure speculation, because Hyalmar Anderson more likely than not died alone.

The investigating party detailed the scene and then placed explosives under the stricken aircraft so that nothing of value would fall into hostile hands. They removed the Norden precision bombsight (a mechanical device used to aim bombs) from the aircraft, recovered the five bodies of the crewmembers, and then moved offshore as the explosives destroyed what was left of the Ventura. Once out in the harbor, they dropped the bombsight over the side of their ship in more than 100 fathoms of water. The Norden bombsight was one of America's top secrets during the war, allowing for high-precision bombing, and it was simply not worth the risk of being compromised. The Navy returned the remains of the five deceased crewmembers to their families, as noted in a brief article in the *Oak Harbor Island County Farm Bureau News* dated June 6, 1944. The worst fears of five of the six crewmember's families were confirmed, but the return of the remains allowed them to grieve and lay their loved ones to rest.

That was not the case for the Andersons. While it seemed impossible that Hyalmar could have survived, they still hoped that he had. Perhaps he had found shelter inland and would show up in the town of Winter Harbour. Nevertheless, days and weeks continued to pass. Finally, on January 12, 1945, James Forrestal, Secretary of the Navy, wrote a letter to the Andersons:

> Mr. and Mrs. Joseph A. Anderson
> Rural Farm Delivery #1
> Ogden, Utah
>
> My dear Mr. and Mrs. Anderson:
>
> After a review of the available information, I am reluctantly forced to the conclusion that your son, Joseph Hyalmar Anderson, Aviation Ordnanceman third class, United States Naval Reserve, is deceased. He was officially reported to be missing as of 26 December 1943, when the plane which he had been aboard crashed on Vancouver Island, Canada.
>
> In compliance with Section 5 of Public Law 490, 77th Congress, as amended, the death of your son is presumed to have occurred on 27 December 1944, which is the day following the expiration of twelve months in the missing status.
>
> I extend to you my sincere sympathy in your

sorrow and hope you may find comfort in the knowledge that your son made the supreme sacrifice while in the service of his country. The Navy shares in your bereavement and has felt the loss of his service.

Sincerely yours,
James Forrestal[5]

RUTH BOTEL'S RESEARCH LEADS
TO A MEMORIAL SERVICE 2005

After the recovery of the bodies and the official presumption of death for Hyalmar, the crash of the Ventura flight was largely forgotten. Residents of Port Hardy, BC, knew about it, and many found their way over to the crash site in the years following the end of World War II. Some brought remnants of the aircraft back as souvenirs. Everyone wondered about the mystery of the one survivor whose remains were never found.

More than fifty years after the crash, a budding local journalist and historian, Ruth Botel, decided to investigate the events of December 1943 and June 1944. A childhood memory from her husband, Carl Botel, sparked her interest. Through the years, he recalled a rainy day in 1943 when, as an eight-year old, he had heard the sounds of heavy piston engines characteristic of a large aircraft. He was at a neighbor's lot, where residents were helping clear brush for a new house. The large airplane flew overhead in the clouds, unseen, but apparently flying very low. This was unusual on the northern end of Vancouver Island, so the young boy paid particular attention to it—especially when the aircraft came lumbering by a few minutes later, the sound growing in intensity as it approached at low altitude and then fading as it passed into the distance. Carl remembers this happening three or four times, as if the aircraft crew were looking for something. Eventually the noise stopped altogether and he returned to his other activities. The discovery of the wrecked aircraft six months later caused those who had heard the Ventura flying overhead in December to put the two events together. It was very likely that Captain Cranny had been searching for a break in the clouds that would reveal the Port Hardy Air Force Base where he could land.

When that did not occur, he apparently chose what appeared to be the very smooth, grassy site of Lawn Point. However, although Lawn Point looks like a large, well-groomed golf course from the air, the reality is quite different. It was not suitable for an emergency landing, as evidenced by the fact that an interrupted set of deep ruts was still evident fifty years later. What this meant is that Cranny had tried to set the aircraft down, realized that the ground was not able to support the aircraft's weight, and then tried to pull up. Unfortunately, he failed to gain enough altitude, and crashed into the evergreen trees at the end of the grassy area.

Because no one locally had kept track of what happened after the bodies were recovered in 1944, Ruth Botel struggled to find information about the crash of the aircraft and its occupants. Neither the US Navy nor the Canadian authorities could tell her anything about it. Working much like a detective, she found the official Canadian death certificates of the five crewmembers. With that information in hand, she was able to piece the story together. In 2000, she wrote a letter to each of the families of the deceased crewmembers, asking for information. The letter to the Andersons went to Joseph's namesake, Joseph Hyalmar Anderson, the son of Irvin Anderson, Hyalmar's older brother. He responded enthusiastically to her request for information in a letter dated March 6, 2000. Joe wrote that while he was named in honor of his fallen uncle, his father never told him much about his namesake. "He always said he went down in a plane when he was on a training mission, and they never found his body. . . . It is really quite amazing how little our family knew about what really happened. . . .

Hyalmar's other siblings seemed to think that the plane went down in the ocean."[6]

Eventually, Ruth Botel wrote two articles in the *North Island Gazette* that appeared on Wednesday, June 1, and Wednesday, June 8, 2005, just prior to a memorial service at the crash site held in honor of Hyalmar.[7] An account of the memorial service appeared in *Contrails*, the official newsletter of the Royal Canadian Air Force 101st Squadron, which went out of its way to make this a special day for the Andersons. Here is an excerpt:

> For a few gentle hours during the morning of June 22nd, 2005, on a remote beach off the northwest coast of Vancouver Island and with the strains of a Scottish lament playing on the bagpipes, the Air Force Ensign flew in the breeze. On the sandy stretch where human footprints are rarely seen, a dozen Americans quietly strolled, some searched the near-impenetrable jungle close to shore. They had come to pay their respects to a loved one who had perished sixty-two years earlier after surviving the crash of a US Navy Ventura patrol bomber back in the dark days of WWII. Lost in a winter storm in 1943 and running low on fuel the pilot was hoping to find the airport at Port Hardy. Instead he glimpsed a deceptively green and level stretch of land—Lawn Point—near the mouth of Quatsino Sound, and attempted to land. We'll never know what happened exactly but for some reason after his wheels touched down he aborted the landing but didn't have enough speed to clear the trees and crashed. The crew survived and desperately waited to be rescued. When searchers finally arrived nearly half a year later there were five bodies neatly arranged under some driftwood. The sixth crewman, Joseph Anderson, was never

found. Now Joe's family had come to find closure and pay their respects.

When 101 Squadron member Lou Lepine heard about the Americans' desire to visit the crash site, he felt the Squadron should do whatever it could to make their visit memorable. Lou immediately set about arranging for a colour party and remembrance service. With the cooperation of 888 (Komox) Wing, the Royal Canadian Legion, Parks Canada, 19 Wing, the Canadian Rangers, and others, 101 Squadron did indeed make the occasion a fitting recognition of brave men who gave their lives in the service of their country.[8]

A year later, the 101st erected a permanent marker at the site. Though missing in action since 1943, Joseph Hyalmar Anderson is no longer forgotten.

A PERSONAL CONNECTION— LLOYD KARTCHNER

I learned of this story from Lloyd Kartchner, a business associate and friend. He invited my wife and me to participate in a 4:00 A.M. memorial service for his uncle Hyalmar Anderson while on an Alaskan cruise in June 2007. While Lloyd never met his uncle, his mother reserved a special place in her heart for her older brother. Here is Lloyd's account of the memorial service:

> There was always an emptiness in my mother's eyes when she talked about her older brother Hyalmar. All the family ever knew was that his plane crashed on Northern Vancouver Island, and that he was never found. Sixty-five years after the family learned of his disappearance, I, and some of my cousins, visited the remote area where his plane crashed. This was a time of healing for our family.

Two years later, I was going to take a cruise from Seattle to Alaska. I knew the cruise route would take us close to Lawn Point where his plane crashed. My uncle had grown up on a dry, sandy hill, and died alone somewhere that was wet and cold. Knowing I would soon pass the last place he spent on this earth, I took a handful of the dry sand from his homestead and put it in a plastic bag. Once on the ship and underway, I contacted the ship's navigational officer and found out when we would pass closest to Lawn Point. At 4 A.M., the next morning, with the outline of Vancouver Island in the background, I and a few close friends held a short memorial service on the stern of the cruise ship. I read the following words that my mom wrote about her brother:

"I think the biggest problem with his death was not knowing what really happened and if he was really gone. War took him from us and gave us nothing in return. All we have are memories of a young man in a navy uniform leaving home with a smile on his face, a hug, and a wave of his hand. He left us saying, 'I'll be seeing you . . .' But he never did."

I slowly dumped the sand from his home place in the ocean. It was sad, but also fulfilling to know that in a small way I had formally honored my uncle Hyalmar, still missing in action after all those years.[9]

MISSING IN ACTION

It is very likely that Hyalmar Anderson could see the lights of civilization from the beachhead where he flew his T-shirt from a pole and attempted to reflect the light of the sun to any passing aircraft. But because of the unique geography of the spot, his attempts failed and he was destined to die alone. Perhaps Emily Dickinson unknowingly wrote his memorial more than 100 years earlier:

Not one of all the purple Host
Who took the Flag today
Can tell the definition
So clear of victory
As he defeated—dying—
on whose forbidden ear
The distant sounds of triumph
Burst agonized and clear![10]

In this respect, Hyalmar is representative of the tens of thousands of other Missing in Action soldiers whose families are left to wonder at their absence. It is a special kind of sorrow.

CHAPTER 4

JOSEPH MEDICINE CROW
THE LAST WAR CHIEF

I n the old tribal days, a Crow warrior had to perform four types of war deeds, four 'coups,' in order to become a chief. The most important, the most respected coup was to sneak into an enemy camp at night and capture a prized horse, perhaps a buffalo horse, a warhorse, even a parade horse. The daring warrior had to slip into the camp unnoticed and find such a valued horse in front of the owner's teepee. . . . That coup is called 'capturing a horse.'

"Another coup was to touch the first enemy to fall in a battle. When warriors from two tribes fought each other, the first person knocked off his horse became a trophy, and warriors from the other side attempted to reach that fallen warrior and touch him with a hand, a riding whip, or maybe the tip of a bow. Sometimes warriors carried a special wand for touching the enemy. This wand—called a coup stick—was wrapped in fur and adorned with eagle feathers.

"For a third coup, a warrior could take away his enemy's weapon—his knife, tomahawk, spear, pistol, or bow.

"The fourth type of coup, usually the last requirement, was to lead a successful war party. After a warrior had completed the first three coups, sometimes several of each, and had proven himself a good, promising warrior, he would be given the opportunity to lead others into danger. If the war party was successful, if it returned with horses and other trophies and if all the warriors returned home safely, the leader of the war party received credit for a coup.

"These were the four coups that a Crow warrior had to accomplish in order to become a chief. There were no shortcuts. Each coup involved risking one's life."[1]

Most Crow warriors carried out their coups against competing tribes or against the US Cavalry in the American Plains wars. Joseph Medicine Crow was to face his four coup attempts as an American Army private during World War II.

Medicine Crow's fascinating story includes his hearing firsthand accounts from his grandfather who had acted as an Army guide at the Battle of the Little Bighorn (also known as Custer's Last Stand), as well as his own service on the battlefields of Europe. Growing up, Medicine Crow endured extreme prejudice from the white men and women who lived on the reservation and taught at his schools. But through the kindness of a Baptist teacher in middle school, he eventually learned to thrive in school; in 1939, he became the first member of the Crow Nation to receive a master's degree. He was doing postgraduate work in anthropology at the University of Southern California (USC) when he was called to arms in defense of America. A friend in Army recruitment offered him the chance to start out as an officer, qualified because of his college degree, but Medicine Crow said that he wanted to do it the Crow way, which was to start out as a warrior who earns advancement through daring deeds and bravery. "It was the biggest mistake I ever made because the US

Army did not work on the principles of the Crow tribe. I entered the Army as a private and came out a private. I never got another chance to be an officer."[2]

Still, his courage under fire and steady judgment in battle earned him leadership opportunities. One of those opportunities would qualify as one of his "coups."

GROWING UP CROW

Joseph Medicine Crow was born in Montana on October 27, 1913. A visiting Sioux warrior, formerly an enemy of the Crow but now a friend of his grandfather Yellowtail, was invited to give Joseph his spiritual name.[3] The elderly warrior accepted this great honor and indicated that he would name the baby Winter Man, in honor of the fact that seven times he, the Sioux warrior, had attacked the Crows as a youth, always in winter, and been injured each time. Because he did not die, he felt that winter had been good to him, and that it would be a blessing to this boy to carry that name. Thus it was that Joseph Medicine Crow was called Winter through childhood and until the end of World War II.

His father, Leo Medicine Crow, passed away two years after Winter was born, and although his mother later remarried, Winter was raised primarily by his maternal grandparents. His grandfather Yellowtail wanted to raise him in the warrior tradition as much as possible, so he made him run around the outside of the house barefoot, even in the snow. Later, he was required to run without clothing to a spot fifty yards from the house, lie down in the snow, roll over as many times as he could endure, and then return to the house. This was one of the ways his grandfather toughened him. Winter also thought it substantiated the wisdom of his spiritual name.

By the time of Winter's childhood, the Crow nation had been decimated by European diseases. At his birth, there were just 2,000 members of the tribe, divided into ten clans.[4] Winter belonged to the Whistling Water Clan. As a child, he learned of the heroic deeds of his paternal grandfather, Chief Medicine Crow, who lived from 1848 to 1920. Medicine Crow had twenty-two war deeds to his credit, an impressive number in Crow society. He completed the four coups to become a chief many times over. He was also a spiritual man who made three vision quests (the fasting experience that Crow warriors performed to gain spiritual power). As a result, Chief Medicine Crow had visions of the future that came true in the real world. This qualified him as medicine man, which meant he was one with spiritual power. One of Chief Medicine Crow's prophecies was that in 1863 he "had a vision in which he saw a long object coming up the river running on round legs and puffing like a steamboat. The Southern Bighorn Railroad was built along the river in 1893, and Medicine Crow had seen it coming 30 years before."[5] He envisioned the steam locomotive without ever before having seen one.

In another vision, a white man came up from the east and said, "I come from the land of the rising sun, where many, many white men live. They are coming and will in time take possession of your land. At that time you will be a great chief of your tribe. Do not oppose these but deal with them wisely and all will turn out all right."[6]

With such great wisdom, Winter's grandfather won the respect of the tribe, and Winter felt honored to carry his name.

It was also as a child that Winter heard firsthand stories of the Battle of the Little Bighorn from his grandmother's brother. "This made him, in the Indian way, my grandfather. He was the longest lived of the [six] Crow scouts and died in my parents' home in 1927."[7] Winter also met and listened to the stories of four of the other scouts as they talked about Custer, who was known as "Son of the Morning Star" by the Crow. When Custer found himself and his troops surrounded by the Sioux and Cheyenne—historic enemies of the Crow—Custer's Crow scouts advised him not to divide his force because they recognized the superior numbers of the Cheyenne and Sioux. They told him to wait until reinforcements arrived. But Custer did not take their advice and split his 700 men into three groups. This so disgusted the Crow scouts that two of them dismounted and changed from their military clothing. When Custer demanded to know why, they replied to the interpreter, "Tell this man he's crazy! He's no good. Tell him that in a very short time we are all going to be killed. I intend to go to 'the other side of the camp'—to the afterlife—dressed as a Crow warrior and not as a white man."[8] That so infuriated Custer that he ordered the Crow scouts to leave. Shortly thereafter, Custer and the 200 men under his direct command were surrounded and massacred.

Throughout his life, Winter spent time at the old battlefield site and later in life shared his stories with visitors to the site.

EDUCATION

Winter started his education in a Baptist-run school but had an early falling-out with the teacher and so received very little attention. By third grade he still could not speak English or read or write. His grandfather removed him from that school and took him to public school in the village of Lodge Grass. Here he suffered from a great deal of prejudice, with most of the white townspeople asserting that their children should not have to go to school with the Native Americans. "These Indians . . . are dirty and covered with lice. They are so dumb the teachers will have to spend more time with them and neglect our kids."[9] This prejudice continued through elementary and middle school, and the Native Americans knew that if they were out in the town after dark, the white kids would beat them up. Fortunately, Winter's teacher spent time with him to help him catch up, and his innate intelligence helped him come up to his grade level.

By high school, Winter had had enough of the local school and asked to go to boarding school off the reservation. His application was declined, but a local Baptist missionary, the Reverend W.A. Petzoldt, found a place for Winter and fourteen other Crow youth in the Bacone Indian School in Oklahoma. Here, Winter thrived. First, he got to rub shoulders with young Native American students from tribes all over the country, including many that had been historical enemies to the Crow. He found that they had much in common, which formed the basis for lifelong friendships. This is also where he started collecting Crow stories, because the youth from the other tribes asked questions about the Crow, and he had no ready answers.

Winter loved Bacone, where he sang bass in the glee club (which went on out-of-state tours each year), learned to play the piano and saxophone, and joined the school pep band and orchestra. He also played basketball and baseball and ran track and field.

In something of a humorous twist, he worked three summers at boys' camps in New Hampshire and New Jersey where he was assigned to teach Native American lore. It was here that he saw his first canoe and had to quickly learn how to use one since it was assumed by everyone that all Native Americans used canoes. It was also here that he first shot a bow and arrow.

After graduating junior college at Bacone, on the night before he left his home to go to Linfield College in Oregon in 1936, his grandmother did something that left a lasting spiritual impression on Winter, one that sustained him later in World War II:

> My Cheyenne grandmother, Walking Woman, was staying with my parents. As I was putting my suitcase into the car just before sunrise, Walking Woman heard the activity and woke up. She came outside and

asked where I was going. My mother told her that I was going away to college in Oregon. The old woman stood there and looked at me intently awhile. Then she stepped forward and turned me around to face east. As I stood there looking across the Little Bighorn River to the horizon, she burst into song. It was a wailing type song that I had never heard before, but it is something the Cheyennes and Sioux do. I did not know if she was singing or crying. It was kind of a mixture. At the end of the song, she gave the Cheyenne woman's trill. Then she pushed me and said, "Go!" This was the traditional way Cheyenne women had sent their husbands and sons off on the warpath in the old inter-tribal war days.

I can still hear her voice to this day. At Linfield things could get pretty tough, and I was ready to quit many times. I had a hard time with accounting. Genetics was rough too. But then I remembered my Cheyenne grandmother sending me off to war. I would remember that, and I would try again. That memory kept me going through all my school days, and it gave me encouragement during the Second World War, when I was an infantryman in Germany. I could almost feel that dear old lady singing and crying like the day it happened.[10]

OFF TO WAR

After receiving a bachelor's degree at Linfield, Winter transferred to USC. But his studies ended when he received a draft notice. Choosing to start out as an enlisted man rather than as an officer, he was assigned to the infantry. As a Christian, Winter did not seek a traditional Crow vision quest, choosing to pray instead. But he still believed in the traditional sources of spiritual power.

For example, he always carried a white eagle feather given to him by his uncle Tom Yellowtail. It had belonged to a Shoshone sun dance chief and was thought to be endowed with spiritual power. In addition, he painted his arms with a red lightning streak and red ring before each battle. The power of this protection was tested one day in battle. While marching on the side of a narrow valley, an artillery shell exploded right in front of him, killing or wounding half a dozen of the American soldiers near him. Winter was knocked unconscious and woke up far down the side of the cliff. In something of a miracle, he was not seriously hurt, even though everyone around him was. But his helmet was gone, along with his feather and his knapsack. Worse, his rifle was missing, which left him defenseless. As he crawled up the side of the hill he was overjoyed to find his rifle. Then, a little further up, his knapsack, and finally at the top of the hill, his helmet with the feather tucked safely inside. He attributed this good fortune to his traditional beliefs and his grandmother's song.

COUNTING COUPS

Although he didn't set out to achieve the four required coups for chiefhood, a number of events conspired to create opportunities.

First, in the middle of a harsh French winter, Private Medicine Crow was standing next to his commanding officer when the order came for a group of men to cross no-man's-land to get dynamite from the nearest French outpost to use in blowing up German concrete pillboxes on the infamous Siegfried line. His commander told Winter to assemble a team and lead the group. Six of his closest friends volunteered to go with him, which made seven, a lucky number for the Crow. The others in the group, none of whom were Native Americans, affectionately called him Chief. Under his leadership they started to pass through the landmines and hidden bombs. The Germans figured out something was happening and aimed artillery at them, while their own forces laid down covering smoke. In spite of hostile fire, the seven soldiers finally made it to the French, who gave them each a fifty-pound box of dynamite. Now they had to make their way back to their own headquarters, facing treacherous enemy fire as well as having to navigate slippery winter slopes while carrying the unwieldy packages. They couldn't put them over their shoulders and it was too hard to hold them in front, so instinctively, Winter put his wooden box between his knees and slid down the main hill. His men observed this and followed suit. Eventually, they all made it back alive with the dynamite intact. It was used to launch a successful assault against the Germans' large gun emplacements.

While entering a small village in Germany, Winter started moving along a large wall for protection. What he didn't know is that a German soldier was paralleling his movements on the other side of the wall, neither one knowing the other was there. When they came to a gate in the wall, they turned into each other. Reacting quickly, Winter slugged the German in the chin, knocking him down and sending his rifle scooting out of reach. He jumped on the man and started to strangle him when his buddies showed up. They wanted to shoot the German. But the German desperately started yelling, "*Hitler Kaput, Hitler Kaput, nicht gude!*" which meant, "Hitler dead, Hitler dead, no good!" The man was crying in terror as he said this. Winter felt bad for him and so released him, taking him as a prisoner of war.

As the German retreat accelerated, Winter's group followed some SS officers who were fleeing ahead of their own men by riding on some magnificent horses. When the Germans camped that night, Winter asked permission to sneak up and let the horses out of their corral so the Germans couldn't use them to escape the next morning. His officer laughed and gave him permission. So Winter and another man crept up on the animals in the dark, where Winter calmed the best of the bunch and used a rope to tie a Crow double half-hitch under the animal's jaw. Winter mounted the horse Crow style while his partner quietly opened the gate, then they led the horses out of their corral and away from the Germans. Once far enough out of sight, he spontaneously rode around the forty captured horses while singing a Crow praise song. Then he let the horses run free, returning to camp on his captured steed. When the German SS awoke the next morning, they quickly surrendered and Winter rode his horse as his unit moved forward. After a while, his commander told him to dismount since he made too good a target way up there on his horse.[11]

THE FOUR COUPS FOR CHIEF

At the end of the war, Medicine Crow returned home to a warm welcome. At a festival thrown in his honor, he described his exploits in war. As he spoke of his experiences, the elders noted that in his first exploit he had successfully led a war party into enemy territory and returned with a valuable prize, the dynamite. On this mission, there was no loss of life of those under his command. An elder pointed out that this counted as a coup. Not having thought of it that way, Medicine Crow then told of his hand-to-hand combat with the German in the village in which he touched him in first contact and also disarmed him. This counted as two coups. Finally, Winter successfully stole a horse from the enemy right next to their camp without harm to himself or the other fellow with him. To his great surprise and pleasure, Joseph Medicine Crow was declared a chief! All in the crowd gave him an ovation and his mother and stepfather passed out gifts to as many as they could—a tribal custom in which someone who is honored gives gifts rather than receiving them.

Joseph Medicine Crow was the last warrior to earn the distinction of being declared a Crow chief. He was also given a new name in honor of his accomplishments, High Bird, along with an honor song. The words of the song are, "High bird, you are a great soldier. High Bird, you fought the mighty Germans. High bird, you counted coup on them. High bird, you are a great soldier."[12] When this honor song was played at this and subsequent events, High Bird led a dance, followed by his family. "The words in my honor song, like the song of the Crow chiefs before me, reflect the pride we Crow people cherish to this day for our warrior heroes."[13]

NATIVE AMERICANS IN WORLD WAR II

More than 25,000 Native American men served in the armed forces in World War II: 21,767 in the Army, 1,910 in the Navy, 874 in the Marines, and 121 in the Coast Guard. This represented up to 70 percent of eligible men in some tribes. Unlike African Americans, who were segregated into separate units, the Native Americans served in integrated units with white soldiers. Since most white Americans believed that Native Americans were excellent warriors, they were quite well accepted into the integrated units, where they fought with distinction.[14]

This chance for so many young men to serve among the whites increased their post-war economic opportunities by providing training and experience. Some believe it was the beginning of an exodus from the reservations and integration into the broader society generally.

In addition to the honors bestowed by the Crow Nation on Chief Joseph Medicine Crow, he was awarded the Bronze Star by the Army and Legion of Honor by the French for his service in World War II. He also received the Presidential Medal of Freedom in 2009 from President Barack Obama. His books include *Counting Coup: Becoming a Crow Chief on the Reservation and Beyond*, written with Herman J. Viola, and *From the Heart of the Crow Country: The Crow Indians' Own Stories*. They are eminently readable and provide wonderful insights into the lives of Native Americans living in the twentieth century. As an historian, Chief Medicine Crow had an easy way with words and stories.

Joe Medicine Crow (High Bird on ceremonial occasions) lived into his 103rd year, passing away in Billings, Montana, on April 3, 2016.[15] He was a distinguished representative of two great nations— the Crow Nation and the United States of America.

CHAPTER 5

DICKEY CHAPELLE
AMERICAN JOURNALIST

Until World War II, female journalists were something of a rare breed, particularly on the battlefield. They were more often writers of books and magazines articles. Even then, it was sometimes difficult for a woman to be taken seriously. Mary Anne Evans was one of the most successful authors of the Victorian era, with most of her seven novels being turned into movies in the twentieth century. But few would recognize her by that name, since she chose to be published as George Eliot, whom most readers presumed to be a male author. Even today, a friend of mine who is a successful author of military fiction writes using her initials because her publishers feel that sales will be higher if her gender is obscured.

Early pioneers in female journalism were few, but included Margaret Fuller, who reported on the Italian revolutions of 1848 and 1849 for the *New York Tribune*; Jane Swisshelm, who spent time volunteering in Union military hospitals in the Civil War and also reported on conditions there; Anna Benjamin, who in 1898 went to Cuba and the Philippines to report on the Spanish-American War; and Mary Roberts Rinehart, who went to Europe in the late fall of 1914 to report on the opening days of World War I for the *Saturday Evening Post*. Rinehart did not confine herself to hospitals, but rather went right out to the front:

"The barbed wire barrier tears my clothes," she wrote in a magazine article. "The wind is howling fiercely. . . . No man's land lies flooded—full of dead bodies." As Rinehart made her way back to safety, she reported, "My heavy boots chafe my heel, and I limp. But I limp rapidly. I do not care to be shot in the back."[1]

Nellie Bly was also a correspondent in the Great War, writing for the *New York Evening Journal* directly from the front lines.

By World War II, acceptance was greater, and the armed services went to great lengths to accommodate the press corps in forward engagements. They accepted that accurate reporting from the front (though often censored to protect military operations) was an important component of keeping morale high at home. The list of distinguished female reporters of the time is extensive. This chapter focuses on one who was particularly bold in going right out to the front in all of America's conflicts from World War II through Vietnam. She is representative of the bravery and skill of the people who place their lives at risk to bring us the news, even in the heat of battle.

DICKEY CHAPELLE

Almost every story about Dickey Chapelle starts with her experience as an accidental combat photographer on the Japanese island of Iwo Jima in World War II and concludes with the story of her death in combat in Vietnam. One of the first female combat photographers, Chapelle earned the respect and admiration of the troops with whom she served in World War II, the Cold War,

Africa, Korea, and the rice paddies of Vietnam. Her bravery was astonishing. Her ability to capture haunting images on film as well as her flair for the written word made her contribution to the military press corps unique. She served her country from behind the camera by documenting the bravery of those who defend freedom, as well as making painfully clear the price they pay in doing so. Her photos and stories were viewed and read by millions.

While it is essential to Chapelle's story to cover the events at the beginning and end of her career (Iwo Jima and Vietnam), to focus on them exclusively misses so much that went on before and in between. Dickey Chapelle is easily one of the most interesting people in the history of war. Her story started in 1919 in Milwaukee, Wisconsin, when Georgette Louise Meyer was born. It was after her marriage and choosing the new first name Dickey that she became Dickey Chapelle.

INTELLIGENT, QUICK WITTED, AND EASILY BORED

Although she was an excellent student, completing four years' worth of high school in just three years, Chapelle loved physical activity more than academics. Her freshman girls' soccer team handily beat the next class up and then had the effrontery to challenge the boys to a game. The school stopped that, but Dickey "knew we could have won it."[2] She wrote of a movie about Admiral Richard Byrd's first expedition to the South Pole: "It hypnotized me. I came home in a daze and announced that I was going to be an aerial explorer."[3] Few men, let alone women, had such grand ambitions in the 1920s, but Chapelle was determined.

After acceptance to both the Massachusetts Institute of Technology (MIT) and Purdue University, she chose MIT because she loved technology. She would have done well there, if not for the airfields near the school. She was attracted to aviation like a moth to a flame, and soon she skipped a chemistry test to take her first flight as a freelance reporter. Heavy flooding was isolating the city of Worcester, Massachusetts, and a relief aircraft was flying badly needed supplies there. Chapelle convinced the pilot to let her ride along to write about the disaster and the relief efforts. The regular reporter for the *Boston-Evening Traveler* was landlocked, so Dickey was first on the scene. During the actual dropping of large crates filled with bread, she was in the copilot's seat, awed by the beauty of flight. It was kismet; Dickey had discovered her destiny as a reporter. Her story about the mission was published in the *Traveler,* and she had discovered the means by which she could support herself: writing action-oriented stories. From that point on, she was never far from the airfield. Two years later, MIT requested that she drop out for lack of attendance and failing grades.

After returning to Milwaukee, she was restless. To relieve the anxiety, she went to the airshows that frequented the Curtiss-Wright Airfield near her home. She thrilled at the aerial acrobatics of the flyers and the daring of the parachutists. After a time, she offered her services as a typist and secretary to the flyers in exchange for flying lessons. "I was the least-promising flight student who ever near-crashed a trainer on each circuit of the field. I was so near-sighted that not even with new prescription lenses in my glasses could I be trusted to judge height, speed or distance. My piloting has never improved much."[4] But still, she could fly, and so she reported with firsthand experience that added authenticity and authority to her writing.

In an effort to save her from a life of grease and danger, her parents asked her to move to Florida with her grandparents, where there were no airshows, airmen, or airfields. But their hopes for her to live a traditional life were short-lived. While on an errand for her grandmother, she spied a poster advertising the Tenth Annual Miami All-American Air Maneuvers, one of the largest air shows in the country.

Chapelle found a job typing press releases for the show's press agent. Her grandmother sighed, and her grandfather visited to affirm that she really would be paid for her work. They both acknowledged that there simply was no chance of her leading a normal life. After helping organize this airshow, her boss asked her to go to Havana, Cuba, as chaperone of six beauty queen winners, even though Dickey was only eighteen years old. "You look older than they do," he said. It was in Havana that she witnessed her first airplane crash, when the chief of the Cuban Air Corps, Captain Manuel Orta, tried to match the skill of the American stunt aviators in a military aircraft ill-suited to acrobatics. His aircraft was smashed beyond recognition when he failed to pull out of a dive, and by the time Dickey ran to the crash site there was little left of the proud Cuban aviator. She filed a news report of the accident with the *New York Times*, which drew the attention of the publicity department of Trans World Airlines (TWA). They offered her a job and a transfer to New York City. Dickey soon fell in love with the excitement and activity of Manhattan.

But she still loved airplanes. One weekend she went to an airshow to witness the test flight of the awesome new Grumman F-3 fighter plane. Thrilled by what she saw, Chapelle angled to experience a full power dive. The story is wonderful:

> The ranking air-show flier in the group that day was racer Al Williams, [who said],
>
> "Anyway, that's one thing your girls won't be doing. You'll never have the stomach muscles for it." As he strode away, I chuckled to myself. It seemed to me he'd forgotten something. We girls wouldn't need to use muscles or elastic bandages, either. For no aeronautic reason at all, I was wearing a girdle (I'd never had one before) and I was sure it would do exactly the same job—*if* I were going to ride high-G pull-outs. . . .
>
> Quickly, I made up my mind and. . . . sought out

the distinguished figure of LeRoy Grumman, who owned the Grumman Aircraft Company. I asked him if he had ever known of a reporter describing the sensations of a terminal velocity power drive.

He, of course, unerringly read my mind. "If you're looking for a ride in my airplane, why don't you just say so?"[5]

After a bit of banter, and to the dismay of the test pilot, Earl T. Converse, Grumman talked his pilot into taking Chapelle up for a ride. Having already completed a dozen test dives that day at G-forces that few other humans have ever experienced, he was tired, ready to go home, and grumpy:

As I splintered my fingernails on the heavy and unfamiliar buckles, he said to me, "Don't forget to scream."

I gaped. He went on, "When your eyes black out, it'll be from the G. Give your gut a break. Scream, so it'll tighten up. And there's one thing you ought to know about this aircraft. With that second seat cut in, it doesn't handle like the service model. What I'm saying is I can't get it out of a spin. So if it ever falls *into* a spin—are you listening?—if it falls into a spin, you jump quick.

"Don't hold up for anybody to *tell* you to jump. Just go. 'Cause I'm telling you now, I am not waiting for—any—damn—dame. Is that clear?"[6]

It was plenty clear. To see if Dickey had courage, Converse took her up in a steep climb then quickly executed a series of rolls that brought the aircraft right to the edge of an uncontrolled spin. When she didn't balk, he decided to give her an easy dive to get her off his back. That went fine, so he treated her to a second graceful drive, asking if she'd had enough.

I understood only that the maneuver we'd just done was all the airplane ride I was going to get, and I knew I couldn't make a story out of it that Mr. Grumman or anyone else would want to read. But I was stymied at how to communicate my disappointment to Connie. Meaning simply what-you-just-did-isn't-good-enough, I set my thumb at the base of my nose and waggled my fingers.

My message was not the one Converse understood. He considered he was being needled, that a woman was offering moral insult to either his flying ability or his aircraft. It didn't matter which. None of his training in combatant response went to waste in that moment. He charged up to twelve thousand feet, slammed the *Woman* into a straight-down power dive, hit terminal velocity almost at once and held it till he had to pull out at nine full G.

There was enough sensation for any writer.

In the dive, the sheer roar of wind and engine was the loudest noise in the history of the world. I measured our speed not as the earth went by but as it grew larger before my eyes. The airport successively was a postage stamp, a handkerchief, a table top, a lawn, a flying field, all the universe existent and—*too close!*

I knew we couldn't pull out any more—I could see the propeller blade of Captain Orta's shattered [aircraft].

But I wasn't dead. Ahead of us came a flash of light from the horizon, not only the darkness of earth. Then, as the pressure drove the blood from my eyes, it all turned black and I could feel the other effects of the terrifying G. The flesh on my cheeks pulled into dewlaps, my calves were stretched like rubber toward my heels, I could not move a muscle of my arms and legs.

Finally I remembered to scream but what I screamed or if I made a sound I could not tell.

Then the plane was straight and level as if it had always been that way. Connie looked around again. "Was that better?" he shouted.

I raised my hands over my head—it felt so good to lift them!—and shook them.

When we landed and Connie at last cut the engine in front of the hangar, the silence was shocking. I realized I was much too weary to climb out of the airplane.

Himself not quite steady, Connie climbed from his seat to the wing. He started wordlessly to lift me bodily to my feet. I found I could stand after all.

I let the parachute fall off me onto the concrete apron and decided to make the great effort involved in speaking two words. *Thank you.* I heard my voice say them and then blindly started home. I know I made it but I don't remember how.

If anyone wants the clinical details of an overdose of G, I'll be happy to spare them finding out the hard way. The symptom is monumental weariness lasting from Sunday evening until Wednesday noon. By then I had the strength to hurl my $3.98 girdle into the wastebasket and compose myself to write. I began with a mental note in big letters to myself:

RE NAVY PILOTS DO NOT I SAY AGAIN NOT NEEDLE IN FLIGHT.[7]

What marvelous storytelling! It's no wonder that Chapelle's freelance writing was picked up by influential magazines, newspapers, and syndicates, including *Look, Life,* and the *New York Times.* And all of this by age nineteen.

TONY CHAPELLE

As part of her work at TWA, Dickey fell under the tutelage of the firm's lead publicity photographer, Tony Chapelle. Tony had been one of the first Navy photographers in World War I. "That made him (when you are nineteen you stop to figure these things out) *at least forty!*"[8] She continued, "He was not as tall as he seemed; authority gave him height to me. He was chunky, with a lot of brown hair and a dark mustache and large animated brown eyes. He moved fast for such a broad man and spoke in a deep melodious voice. He had the most cheerful disposition of anyone I had ever known—except when he was initiating tyros into the mysteries of the one matter on earth he held utterly sacred, photography."[9]

She was awestruck by her instructor. So much so that "in October of 1940, the teacher and I went out to Milwaukee, and in front of a bank of gladiolas from my mother's garden, we were married."[10]

Tony taught Dickey everything she needed to know to become a world class photographer. Not that she was at first; hauling around the heavy Speed Graphic newspaper camera took physical stamina and careful thought to properly set up a picture. There was no point-and-shoot in those days; the camera was simply too bulky to get off candid shots. So a photographer had to picture the shot first in his or her mind and then maneuver the equipment into position to get the desired effect. When the situation called for quick action, the photographer who won the day was the one who had anticipated in advance where he or she needed to be:

> If you were a real photographer, you kept your equipment ready to shoot. Anywhere on earth at any time, you reloaded with fresh film and labeled and stored the exposed supply before you went to sleep. First thing the next morning was always too late, according to Tony. . . .

If you were a real photographer, you were on the spot where things happened beforehand. You did not walk to airplane crashes, Tony told me scornfully, recalling my story of Captain Orta's death [in Cuba]. "You're sitting on the fire truck before the airplane hits [the ground] and nobody takes time to throw you off so you get out there ahead of the police. *Ahead.*" . . .

If a picture was a failure, no alibi would placate Tony. If your equipment failed, it was because you hadn't taken proper care of it. If you weren't in the right position to shoot, it was because you were too lazy to have climbed up where you should have been. And if your nerve failed—but then, I'd been a photographer for ten years myself before I ever heard one admit he'd been too shaken to shoot. Joe Rosenthal said it happened to him during the battle of the Philippine Sea. To make up for his lapse, he went on to shoot the most famous news photograph in history, the flag raising on Iwo Jima.[11]

Dickey was initially rejected by the major magazines, so Tony patiently taught Dickey to make a sample story of her photographs by finding a human-interest story and then pursuing it until she could select from hundreds of photographs:

Out at the Brewster aircraft plant in Newark, New Jersey, Margie Alsvary sewed the fabric onto the wings of RAF [Royal Air Force] fighter planes on their way to be flown in the battle of Britain. Each working day for three weeks, I went across the Hudson to the Brewster plant trying to make a set of pictures which would show her life throughout every hour of one day. Each night Tony and I would process the pictures and decide the set was still incomplete—if you counted only the *good* pictures.

But the day finally came when even Tony admitted the set was as good as I could make it. I took it to *Look*—and they bought it! I saw my first story in print, a big pix-page layout. For the next six months, I tried to repeat my triumph. I photographed aviation events, bicycle racers, a tomato-and-lettuce sandwich sequence for a drug company. Occasionally I sold a picture—usually a single print to a newspaper. At last *Look* bought two layouts in a single day, one showing a Canadian pilot's holiday in New York and the other a series of photographs showing Alma Heflin at work.[12]

At this time, *Look* magazine had a circulation of approximately two million readers, who appreciated learning events of the day primarily through photos with brief supporting text. Dickey Chapelle was quickly establishing herself as both a writer and a photographer. She would soon have to choose between the two.

AMERICA ENTERS WORLD WAR II

With America's entry into World War II on December 7, 1941, Tony Chapelle reenlisted in the Navy and was quickly assigned to Panama to train high-altitude reconnaissance photographers. Dickey rather cleverly got herself assigned to Panama as a credentialed photographer for *Look*, ostensibly to photograph the training of the Fourteenth Infantry Regiment. But it also allowed her to be the only military wife left in Panama—the others having been sent home. She and Tony spent nearly a year together before the military brought an end to it by transferring Tony back to Long Island in New York City. Dickey completed her assignment and returned home as well.

When it looked like Tony was to be transferred to Chungking (now known as Chongqin), China, to set up a photo center for propaganda purposes in late 1944, Dickey decided she wanted to go closer to the action as well. She applied for a magazine assignment to the Pacific theater. "Ten days later, Tony faced what must surely be the most awkward moment in a husband's life. His own orders inexplicably delayed, he had to say good-bye to his wife while she went off to war."[13] Dickey was sponsored in this new assignment by Fawcett Publications, who hired her to represent two of their most popular magazines, *Woman's Day* and *Popular Mechanics*.

Because it was vital to keep the home-front morale high, the War Department allowed the press to pay the salary of their wartime correspondents but mandated that the expenses of travel, food, and housing be covered by the Army, Navy, or Air Force. Dickey said, "The services give this cooperation so the correspondent will at least be able to write stories useful to the prosecution of the war as well as satisfactory to his [or her] editors."[14] The only requirement imposed on the press was that they had to take orders from the military commanders in the area. In exchange, the custom was to treat each correspondent as a kind of junior officer, calling this granted status a "simulated rank." In 1945, they were given the simulated rank of captains in the Army and lieutenant commanders in the Navy.[15]

JOURNALIST OR PHOTOGRAPHER?

Arriving in Oakland, California, Dickey Chapelle reported to the Navy liaison officer to the press corps. He asked her if she was to be credentialed as a photographer or as a reporter. She told him she would be both since her magazines had no one else in the area. "'You can't be both,' he told me firmly. 'On operations, you may use radio facilities if you are a writer, or your camera if you are a photographer, but only one.'" This posed a dilemma for Chapelle, which she resolved by asking how many accredited women writers and photographers there were. When she heard that there were several writers but no photographers, she replied, "'I'm a photographer, then.'" This was a choice that would define her for the rest of her life. When asked where she wanted to go, she replied with a phrase that would soon become her trademark, "'As far forward as you'll let me.'" In her usual enthusiastic way she later wrote, "Once I'd said it, I was delighted with the way the sentence rang and echoed, like a bell. I expected it would get me to Honolulu, anyway. I knew this was the most advanced station for WACS and WAVES."[16]

Her guess was right. The very next day she boarded a military aircraft with a score of Navy flight nurses on their way to Hawaii. But that was only the beginning. When she landed in Honolulu, she was asked where she wanted to go and again she replied, "'As far forward as you'll let me.'"[17] Very soon she was on a hospital ship sailing to the Japanese island of Iwo Jima, the site of some of the hottest and most gruesome fighting of World War II. On the way, her hospital ship came under attack by a Japanese pilot in violation of the Geneva Convention. Remembering her training from Tony, she raced to a spot on the highest part of the ship and it was there that she lodged herself with her camera as the Japanese aircraft made its final approach to destroy the ship. With camera ready, and fully aware that it could drop its bomb right into the superstructure below her, Chapelle prepared herself to take the shot. Fortunately, a US Navy destroyer fired at the Japanese aircraft at just the last moment before it released its bomb, forcing it to veer off without completing its mission of destruction. Dickey Chapelle was in combat!

When the hospital ship the USS *Samaritan* dropped anchor near Iwo Jima, Dickey quickly learned the true nature of war as 551 critically wounded Marines were brought on board—100 more than the ship's rated capacity. It was also in these first moments on the edge of battle that she learned the great capacity for humans to endure. After reflecting on the fact that words were simply inadequate to convey the scenes of battle, she wrote:

It's my feet that remember the blood. A pool of blood was something a man left behind him on the deck like his gun and his pack. The important thing about the blood was that it was slippery under your feet, and you had to be careful if you were standing in it not to fall down when the ship rolled.

None of these impressions, though, is as unfading as what the heart remembers. This is the eternal, incredible, appalling, macabre, irreverent, joyous gestures of love for life, the fact of life, made by the wounded.

When I first began to work on the welldeck, I tried only to keep out of the way of the stretcher-bearers and to keep focusing, framing, lighting and shooting pictures. The shapeless dirty bloody green bundles being lifted and carried before me were not *repeat not* human as I was human. Some part of my mind warned me that if I thought of them as people, just once, I'd be unable to take any more pictures. Then the story of their anguish would never be told since there was no one else here to tell it.

A corporal named Martin from Scranton destroyed that defense in two minutes flat. He wasn't only shapeless and bloody and foam-lipped; he was dying when he reached the hospital ship. . . .

Because his was the only stretcher not likely to be moved for a few minutes, I squatted beside it to change the film in my camera. I hadn't looked at the face of any hurting man except through the finder of the camera yet. Now, shyly, without the square of wire between us, I looked at his. His eyes had opened and rested on the white pipes overhead. The cardboard tag reading URGENT . . . obscured his chin and lay across his lips. I reached over and folded it back so it wouldn't impede his breathing. *God, he doesn't want to die!*

He saw me now and the deep lines in his face changed. He was trying to smile![18]

Dickey then asked him how he felt and he replied that he was a "Ma-rine. I'm a [expletive] Marine." This made Dickey smile, and she thought he would smile again if she said it back to him. So she did, challenging him that he still hadn't told her how he felt.

> "I—feel—luck-y."
> I looked up at the blood bottle hanging over his arm and back at what was left of his legs and then to his face with the big M on the forehead which meant he had been injected with morphine. What in the name of all that was holy did he have to feel lucky about? "Because—I'm here. Off—the beach."
> I still didn't say anything. I knew he ought not to waste his strength talking even though the transfusion was reviving him. But he went on.
> "There's—another thing. I—I always knew the guys in the squad liked me, see?" He stopped now because something hurt. But then his face was controlled again, and he picked up smoothly. "But I never knew—the guys cared enough to get me—the hell out of there. When I got it they did. Three miles they carried me. Makes a guy feel lucky." He positively grinned now as if he saw them on deck with us and he wanted them to know he had come through to safety. . . .
> After that, I looked squarely at each Marine as I photographed him. As the hours passed, I learned that the one thing almost every man who could talk said was just what Martin had said.
> I'm lucky. I am alive. I am here.[19]

Shortly after her remarkable encounter with Martin, she took a photograph of man named Johnny, who had lost a great deal of blood. The next morning, he cheerfully called to her that she had taken his picture. But she had no recollection. She even bet him that she had not but handed him her journal and said that if he could find the numbers from his dog tag she would certainly be surprised. He found them almost immediately. How could she have photographed a face and not recognize it so soon after? She asked a corpsman (Navy medic) about it. "We don't recognize him this morning either," he replied. He then explained that Johnny had been bleeding for five hours before being brought on board the hospital ship, and that his heartbeat was almost imperceptible. When they started blood transfusions, his wound wouldn't clot until they had transfused fourteen pints of blood—nearly twice the amount the human body can hold. He was unconscious through all of this. When he awoke the next morning, he was vital and cheerful, his face completely transformed. The corpsman then said, "If anybody ever asks you, does the blood out here do any good—you just tell them about Johnny." Dickey nodded, then went back and told Johnny what had happened, much to his astonishment. She then took a follow-up photo. "For the next ten years, that pair of pictures, taken only twenty-four hours and fourteen pints of blood apart, were used to spur blood donor drives all over the country. I tried to send each new poster to Johnny's mother in Waycross, but there were too many reproductions of the pictures and I lost track."[20]

This incident shows the power of photography to tell a story in a moment and to move people to action and compassion.

From Iwo Jima, Dickey Chapelle went on to the island of Guam and then, when asked where she wanted to go, replied, "'As far forward as you'll let me.'" That took her to Okinawa, the only woman reporter on a hospital ship in the invasion fleet. When the fleet arrived, Dickey was under orders to remain onboard to continue to cover the rescue of the wounded. But in the early hours of the invasion there were no wounded; the Japanese were holding back until the Americans landed. So she maneuvered to get her orders changed. That is how she found herself on the beach at Okinawa just as the fighting began. Rough weather had come up at sea so she couldn't be evacuated; instead she hunkered down and watched as the furious battle unfolded. Japanese pilots made kamikaze attacks on the ships offshore while the ships fired furious fusillades behind enemy lines to soften up the Japanese resistance. It was a battle unlike anything in her experience. Not aware that her presence on the island was causing consternation to senior command, she next made her way to a field hospital. Here she assisted a surgeon performing chest surgery by holding a flashlight during the operation. Anything brighter would have attracted the enemy, so for more than two hours she held the light aloft as the surgeon worked to save the Marine's life. When it was finished, her arms wouldn't stop shaking from the strain, but the Marine was breathing normally. She had helped to save a life.

After many other forays up to the front, almost always under fire, Dickey learned an important lesson about fear:

> The chief relaxed into his usual mocking manner, "Scared?" he asked.
>
> "I'm not sure. . . . That's something I wanted to talk with you about."
>
> The chief looked uneasy again as if he wanted to say he was not serving the United States Marine Corps to provide free psychoanalysis to a dame in the middle of a shooting war. What he did say was,
>
> "Okay, but don't start to crawl in my lap. I'm just as scared as you are."
>
> I didn't joke back. I told him I couldn't understand why I was so often frightened at the wrong time. "I get scared much worse when I'm mixed up than when something is really dangerous. It's as though the [enemy] didn't have anything to do with what scares me."

The chief seemed to be waiting for me to go on. Finally, he said, "Well?"

"Well, what?"

"Well, you got it all figured out for yourself."

"No, I haven't," I objected.

"Sure, you have. You just said it. What makes the difference is not what anybody else does. It's what *you* do, what *you* think. Look, Dickey—" he leaned over again . . . making each word distinct. "Sure, the [enemy] can kill you. You light a butt out here after dark and you won't live to finish smoking it. That's easy to figure.

"But only you can get yourself all shook up about it. Instead, a person can go on doing what needs to be done, like me giving a transfusion or you taking a picture. It's not for anybody else to decide what happens in your own mind; you have to choose yourself.

"Sure, they can kill you. But—that's—all—they can do. Only you can frighten you."

Only I can frighten me. I said it slowly out loud because it was a brand new idea. I didn't guess then how many times in my life I would repeat it.[21]

Shortly after this, Dickey was riding on a jeep looking for wounded Marines when a Marine sentry held up his hand to stop the jeep. Coming around, he told Dickey that she shouldn't put the military police through this anymore. She replied that she'd never met him and certainly never asked anything of him. "'That's right,'" replied the Marine. "'You didn't. But they come on the radio two, three times every day to find out if we've seen you. There's an arrest-on-sight order out for you—well, the first way we got it, it was shoot-on-sight, but I guess that was a mistake in transmission. Today you've driven by here three times already and I'm going to get myself in a bind if you keep on doing it.'"[22]

Dickey knew that she was at risk for having come ashore under dubious circumstances but was not prepared for an arrest order. She wondered what she had done. The Marines had no idea; they just ordered her to return to her ship. Once onboard, she was told that she had embarrassed an admiral. This discussion was cut short by a fierce kamikaze attack—the first of many against the ship in the next seventy-two hours. She wrote, "No experience in combat which I have ever known is quite like standing before *kamikazes*, feeling the incredible relentless paralysis at the sight of a fellow human being in the dive which must inevitably end in at least his own death. The attacks seemed a grisly roulette, the black dot of the plane falling and skipping among the blue squares of the sea and the gray squares of the warships decks."[23] Fortunately, her ship was never hit and she made it safely back to Guam. There she was reminded that the admiral himself had ordered her not to go on shore at Okinawa. She had neglected to mention this to his field officer on site in Okinawa when she asked permission. Having a woman in the forefront of battle was considered a risk to all Marines since it was in their nature to protect her, even if it meant risking and losing their own lives to do so. For her impudence, she was stripped of her credentials and sent back to the United States. Her service in World War II was at an end.

HUMANITARIAN PHOTOGRAPHERS

Once home in America she was quickly fired by her magazine. They found her pictures too grisly and the men too "dirty" to print. This enraged Dickey Chapelle, since she thought it a small price for readers to pay to see that Marines in the field got dirt on their uniforms. Fortunately for history, *Cosmopolitan* magazine published many of her undoctored photos a few months later, thereby paying tribute to the actual suffering of men in combat.

She and her husband then went to work for various humanitarian and relief agencies, taking photos that could move people to support just causes. Their efforts focused on the urgent need to relieve the suffering of Europeans whose homes and industries had been devastated by war. They traveled to nearly every country in Europe. Sometimes they worked with a team of Quakers; while on other assignments, they worked for CARE, the United Nations International Children's Emergency Fund (UNICEF), and the Save the Children Federation. The Chapelles made very little money on these ventures but felt buoyed by the impact they had on people's lives. Their work as a husband-wife team became featured human-interest stories in the *New York Herald Tribune*, the *Christian Science Monitor*, and the *New York World-Telegram*. In this way, they helped to raise millions of dollars to alleviate Europe's suffering.

But the strain of their lifestyle took a toll and Tony and Dickey's collaboration, and their marriage, ended in 1953. She later wrote:

> Several times television interviewers and people who hear me lecture have asked me the same question about marriage. Can a woman be both a foreign correspondent and a wife?
>
> My answer is—never at the same time.
>
> I can't make the reason sound sentimental although I'm sure it has to do with the heart and not the head. But good correspondents are created out of the simple compulsion to go see for themselves what is happening. There's competition for their assignments, and the odds are heavily in favor of the man or woman who yields to the fewest distractions in obeying the compulsion. It's a twenty-four-hour a day task till a story's done and you cannot know as you start covering an event where it may lead you. Till it's done, people you love always receive less evidence of love than the correspondent wants to give them. My mother's formula that human problems are solved by

loving more—and in no other way—is, I'm sure, the correct one. Some marriages survive this deprivation indefinitely but mine (and most of them) did not.[24]

She paid a heavy price for the causes she served. Her father passed away in 1954 and her mother in 1956. She was now alone.

TAKEN PRISONER BY THE COMMUNISTS

After many years of aid work, Dickey went to work for a commercial venture, the Research Institute of America. Her job was to publicize their studies. But in 1956, *Life* magazine needed a correspondent to go behind the Iron Curtain into communist Hungary to document the unfolding refugee crisis brought on by the revolution. They asked Dickey, who requested a two-week leave of absence from her regular job. Little did she know that in taking badly needed penicillin into the war zone, she would be captured and taken prisoner. Held in Budapest against her will while demanding a chance to meet with the American consul, she found herself imprisoned on a meager diet that left her very close to starvation. She soon learned that her jailers controlled her with food. She also concluded that it was not the intent of those who tortured and interrogated her and her fellow prisoners to "brainwash" them with false memories or loyalties, but rather to break their will. To accomplish this, her captors kept Dickey in solitary confinement where she spent many days without seeing another human being other than occasional interruptions to meet with her interrogators. After five weeks alone she was bereft:

> It is a curious and awful time.
> Here is a universe unpeopled. Walled-in not just by brick, but by ends—ends of sensation, and of plan, and of movement. You sense that there can be no beginnings here.

The most important thing about it is that it hurts.

I first strung those few sentences together in my mind in the solitary cell and I put them down only a few days after I came out of prison. When I reread them weeks later, I found that my body remembered more vividly than my brain. My shoulders tensed till they ached, my hands grew cold, my throat clenched with nausea.

The awareness of being starkly alone can swell like a true sound, a dissonance so vast no other hurt is real.

. . . Only the pain of the present is real. Then I would think,—*I've had it; why don't I die?*

There, of course, lay the clue to the one effective resistance:

That I've had it—that's exactly what they want me to think![25]

After months in prison, Dickey Chapelle was brought before a communist Hungarian court to be tried for entering the country without a valid visa. When asked why she had entered Hungary she said to bring a token of relief in the form of penicillin. When asked about the details of her arrest and confinement, she spoke truthfully. Always in the back of her mind was the fact that another American journalist had been imprisoned for two years before being expelled. She had served two seemingly endless months. In a trial where everything was conducted in a language she did not understand, she was ultimately found guilty and sentenced to time served and expulsion from the country. The American consul certified that if he could assume responsibility for her person, he would see to it that she was out of Hungary in fewer than forty-eight hours. This offer was accepted, and Dickey had to return to her cell to gather her belongings. Here she thanked the other prisoners and the few guards who had been kind to her, and then left with a feeling of guilt for leaving them behind.

She remained anxious that her release would be thwarted and her case tied up in bureaucratic maneuvering for many years, a thought that terrified her. Only when the car she was in finally turned onto the grounds of the American embassy did she finally allow herself to think she might actually be set free. American Minister Thomas Wailes stepped forward and took one of her dirty hands into both of his and welcomed her. She was embarrassed by her condition, even more so when the minister's wife, Cornelia Wailes, stepped forward to hug her. Dickey shrunk back, saying that she had been in a cell with a prisoner dying of tuberculosis. "'I don't care,' said the minister's wife, and she put her arms around me and kissed me."[26] After her forced isolation, Dickey finally enjoyed the comfort of human touch.

When she returned to America she was greeted by the Overseas Press Club of New York, which had worked for her release from the moment the Associated Press announced that she was missing. To give meaning to what had happened to her, she set about to write her story. It was ugly reading, but the *Reader's Digest* courageously printed it in English and in a dozen other languages and distributed it in more than 110 countries. Hers was a powerful, critical voice in documenting the cruelty of the Cold War and the snuffing out of freedom by the Communists.

SPECIAL CORRESPONDENT TO THE BAYONET BORDERS OF THE WORLD

Undeterred by her prison experience in Hungary, Chapelle rejected the life of a corporate photographer and again set off to the far corners of the world. By 1959 she had been on assignment in Hungary, Algeria, Lebanon, and South Korea. With her military credentials restored, she traveled to wherever the flames of revolution or resistance burned hottest. When not on assignment, Dickey enjoyed going on the lecture circuit. She enthralled audiences in schools, universities, and in Veterans of Foreign Wars and American Legion halls around America.

Her restless energy and drive eventually took her to the violent fields of South Vietnam. After the French had failed to quell a communist uprising led by North Vietnamese leader Ho Chi Minh, America stepped into the breach, seeing war in Southeast Asia as necessary to stop the spread of communism. Vietnam proved an almost impossible place to wage war, where civilians often acted as saboteurs and the South Vietnamese government was more corrupt than the North. But Dickey was thrilled to be serving once again with her beloved Marines. It was 1965 and Dickey was on assignment for the *National Observer* and RKO Broadcasting Company. She had what was then the rather novel assignment of developing a story around a specific Marine Corps company, following them from training into active combat. That is why she drew so close to the men in the company. She was with them from the beginning. In today's terms, she would be classified as being embedded with this group.

She felt that no combat assignment was too dangerous as she carefully documented the struggles and sacrifices of the men she loved. On November 4, 1965, camera in hand, Dickey did what she had many times before: joined some of the Marines in the company she was following and went out on patrol. It would be her last patrol—in Vietnam and on this earth. A Marine walking ahead of Dickey set off an improvised explosive and a piece of shrapnel hit Dickey in the neck, severing her carotid artery. She became the first female American correspondent to be killed in action. An honor guard of Marines personally escorted her remains back to her home in the United States.

IN MEMORIAM

Dickey Chapelle was gone, but her memory is immortal. Renowned war photographer Henri Huet, who was on the same patrol, snapped a photo of a Navy chaplain performing the last rites for Dickey, who lay dressed in battle fatigues, with her camera by her side. She was buried by her family back in Milwaukee, but with full military honors—a rare tribute for a civilian.[27]

Since her death, Chapelle has been honored by the annual Dickey Chapelle Award awarded each year by the Marine Corps League and the United States Marines. The Milwaukee Press Club inducted their native daughter into their Hall of Fame on October 24, 2014, to honor the fiftieth anniversary of her death. On the exact anniversary of her death, fifty years later (2015), Wisconsin governor Scott Walker declared November 4 "Wisconsin Combat Journalist Day" to honor Chapelle and all the other correspondents who put their lives at risk in combat around the world.[28]

COMBAT JOURNALISTS

Dickey Chappelle's family considered themselves pacifists, opposed to violence and war. Dickey honored that tradition by never taking a life herself. Her story is symbolic of the tens of thousands of journalists who place their lives at risk in dangerous places all around the world and in every conflict in which America has been involved. They too are invisible soldiers—soldiers of truth who honor America's first freedom enshrined in the Bill of Rights: "Congress shall make no law respecting an establishment of religion, or prohibiting the free exercise thereof; or abridging the freedom of speech, or of the press; or the right of the people peaceably to assemble, and to petition the Government for a redress of grievances."[29] Theirs is a noble and dangerous cause.

PART TWO

UNITED ACTS OF HEROISM

CHAPTER 6

NAVAJO CODE TALKERS

HEROES OF THE PACIFIC WAR

Give me courage. Let me make my country proud. Please protect me. Let me live to walk in beauty. . . . In beauty, all is made whole. In beauty, all is restored."[1]

This was the remarkable prayer offered by Chester Nez, a proud member of the Navajo Nation and the United States Army, as he prepared to go into battle for the first time at the Battle of Guadalcanal in the South Pacific. It highlights the deep respect the Navajos have for the earth and the remarkable camaraderie that they enjoyed with each other.

As a child, Chester had been subjected to severe racial discrimination by white teachers, who made a sustained effort to forbid young Navajo students from using their native language. Now, Chester and others like him would use the Navajo language to create and implement an unbreakable secret code used to transmit vital combat intelligence in the Pacific theater of World War II. Nez and his comrades acted as living code machines whose transmissions were never deciphered by the Japanese. They did this using oral radio transmissions in which Navajo words were substituted for letters of the English alphabet or for military words used in combat.

Because Navajo is an extremely complex spoken language, and a complete system of writing had only been developed in the late 1930s and early 1940s and was not in widespread use until decades later,[2] the Japanese had no way to decipher the unique code developed by the original twenty-nine participants in the project. Part of the code's success was attributable to the fact that certain Navajo words are discernible only by the tone and pitch in which they are spoken, and those tones are recognized exclusively by those who learned the language as children. To outsiders, some words that Navajos can differentiate between sound the same. As time passed, the Navajo Marines added additional words to substitute for letters of the English alphabet, which made the code virtually impenetrable to the Japanese. This created great frustration for the Japanese, who had been able to break all previous American codes.

The effectiveness of the Navajo code was quickly demonstrated on its very first day in use. Initially, the communications officer to whom the Navajo code talkers were assigned expressed deep skepticism about using the Navajo Marines to decipher transmissions. He had previously relied on codes being sent mechanically through machines at both ends of the transmission. To justify his continuing use of the mechanical code, the officer ordered a competition between the two. Here is how Chester Nez describes the test:

> Some communications officers on Guadalcanal greeted us Navajos with skepticism.
> . . . My group of code talkers was assigned to just such a doubter, Lieutenant Hunt, signal officer under General Alexander Vandergrift. When we Navajos assigned to him had arrived, Hunt just shook his head.

He knew of our mission, but he had never worked with a group of Indians, and he had faith in the old code. Also, he was one of the officers who hated the idea of switching tactics in the middle of a major military operation.

He had decided to test the new code immediately and had given us a message to send out on our first night. Directly after the transmission began, panicked calls came in. Hunt's other radio operators jammed our Navajo speech, thinking the Japanese had broken into their frequency. By then it was dark, and the annoyed Hunt postponed the test.

That next morning Lieutenant Hunt continued with the trial of the code. He ordered his radiomen not to jam the transmissions, then told us code talkers to do our best. The test would determine whether or not he could use us! Both the code talkers and the standard communications men were given the same message, one Hunt estimated would take four hours to transmit and receive using the old Shackle protocol.

With the Shackle method, a mechanical coding machine was used to encode a written message. The encoded message was then sent via voice. These encoded messages were a jumble of numbers and letters, and unlike the Navajo code, were meaningless to the person transmitting them. At the receiving end, a cipher was used to decode the message. The entire process was cumbersome and prone to error.

While the men utilizing the Shackle code waited for the encoding machine to accomplish its work, one of our men, I think it was William McCabe, transmitted the message to another code talker. I can't remember who. The message that Hunt had estimated would take four hours by Shackle took only two and a half minutes by Navajo code—an impossible feat by current standards. And the message was transmitted accurately, word for word. Lieutenant Hunt was impressed.

But we Navajo code talkers already knew our code was good. None of us wanted it to go unused. With a code that could keep military plans and movements secret, our country would outmaneuver the Japanese. We were sure of it.[3]

Two and a half minutes instead of four and a half hours! Military intelligence was about to undergo a radical transformation, and the Navajos would see almost continual service in the coming weeks and months of battle, sometimes working twenty-four-hour shifts with very few breaks. By the end of the war in the Pacific, more than 400 young Navajo men had served their country with distinction. But because of the secret nature of their work, nothing could be said of their unique contribution to victory until the program was declassified in 1968.

In battle, their contribution was significant and sometimes decisive. For example, after six code talkers worked virtually around the clock for the first two days of the battle of Iwo Jima, sending and decoding more than 800 messages, Major Howard Connor of the Fifth Marine Division said, "Were it not for the Navajos, the Marines would never have taken Iwo Jima."[4] High praise for men who not only operated the most secure communications system in the world during the heat of battle, but who also fired weapons in combat as active-duty Marines when not needed for coding work. They were invisible heroes, from an unappreciated minority, whose bravery was finally recognized by the United States in the year 2000, when the Congressional Gold Medal was awarded to the original twenty-nine code talkers and the Congressional Silver Medal to the other code talkers who served in active combat. By then, just five of the original twenty-nine were still alive.[5] It's impossible to calculate how many American lives were saved by their efforts.

GROWING UP AS A NATIVE AMERICAN IN THE EARLY TWENTIETH CENTURY

In Navajo life, everything has a story. Chester Nez grew up listening to his father and grandmother retell the Navajo story of the creation (*diné bahane'*). As Chester listened to the story, the Navajo words for light (*'adinídíín*), earth (*nahasdzáán*), water (*tó*), and air (*nitch'l*) were imprinted in his mind. His grandmother reminded him each time she told the story:

> "As these words were spoken, . . . the sun, the earth, the oceans, and the air that we breathe appeared. . . . The spoken Navajo words could not be separated from the physical sun, the actual earth, the oceans and air. Speaking our language created the world, and the creation of the world made our language."[6]

Chester learned to live his life with a deep connection to the earth, under a solemn obligation to find balance in his life, both with nature and with other people. For Chester, the Navajo language was very much a part of this way of life, with a richness and variety that is difficult for outsiders to appreciate. He was taught about the "Right Way," a balanced approach to life that means a person should always seek after beauty and support their friends rather than competing with them. Living the Right Way helped Chester and the other code talkers maintain an even temperament during basic training and later in battle. Because of the demanding physical conditions under which Chester and his fellow Navajo Marines had grown up—often walking or running for dozens of miles—they easily adapted to the physical conditioning routines of the military. And they enjoyed a close and easy companionship with both their

Navajo and white comrades in arms that quickly earned them respect and acceptance.

As both individuals and as members of the communication group, they seldom lost their temper or composure. They simply buckled down to the task at hand, responding to whatever danger presented itself, while working diligently to transmit the urgent messages that were ever present in battle.

Most of the original code talkers grew up in the days between the world wars on, or near, the Navajo and Hopi Nations in the Four Corners area where the states of Utah, Colorado, New Mexico, and Arizona intersect. Chester Nez spent his early life in the Checkerboard area of New Mexico, where alternating sections of land were owned by the Navajos and by their white neighbors. It is a high desert landscape with little water to support agriculture. They lived in what most Americans would consider extreme poverty, with no electricity or running water, in hogans, small cylindrical cabin-like structures made of tree boughs with earthen roofs. As boys, they often experienced hunger and physical privation. Almost no one had cars, trucks, or horses, so walking was the only way to travel.

Yet despite the lack of modern facilities, their families were strong and loving, inculcating the values of their culture deep into the heart and soul of the boys. To support themselves, most Navajo grazed sheep on common land. Navajo society is largely matriarchal, and families were identified by the mother's name rather than the father's.

Relations with the government were always fraught. In 1934, disaster struck the Navajo Nation when the United States Bureau of Indian Affairs decided to cull the sheep herds owned by individual families. The Nez family watched helplessly as more than 750 sheep were slaughtered and the carcasses buried. The goal of the program was to reduce overgrazing and force the Navajo to find new ways to farm. Skeptics thought it was a way to make the Navajo more dependent on the federal government and less independent. Whatever the reason, the result was devastating. Suffering and hunger were rampant, since the government did not step in with enough food to make up for the shortfall. Some families received a small payment of three dollars per sheep; the market price at the time was eight to ten dollars. Many received nothing. In the six years the program was in place, the Navajo herds were reduced from approximately 1.6 million sheep to fewer than 400,000. What was perhaps affected most by the killing off of the Navajo herds was the community spirit of the Navajo. Some families wondered why they should continue to work hard building up their flocks when the government could come in at any time and destroy them, which led some to indolence. Others became self-interested for the first time, giving up the communal sharing of land and putting up fences to protect their smaller flocks.[7]

One positive aspect of the program was that in return for the destruction of the flocks, the government promised to provide education to the young men of the Navajo. This is how most of the 400 code talkers learned to speak fluent English. In the boarding schools, however, the matrons and masters were ruthless in enforcing an English-only policy. The goal was to extinguish their native language so that young Navajo would be forced to assimilate into white society. When the children first arrived at school with no knowledge of English, this English-only policy led to frequent mistakes, which were punished physically, through being beaten or slapped. Most lived in constant fear of being hurt and embarrassed:

> The knowledge of constant danger sat lodged in the pit of my stomach like a rock. I tried my best to answer questions correctly, but never knew when a matron would strike. They watched, their dark cold eyes waiting for us to make a mistake, to do something wrong. I was always afraid.

Snow fell softly outside the dormitory windows. Loud whispering came from two beds away. Navajo. I'd been caught speaking Navajo three days before. The Pima matron brushed my teeth with brown Fels-Naptha soap. I still couldn't taste food, only the acrid, bitter taste of the lye soap.

Teachers at the school were encouraged to be strict, and the smaller children were frequently targeted by slaps or kicks. But the lingering taste of the soap was worse than either of those punishments.

"Why do you think the matrons are so mean?" the small, high voice, speaking in Navajo, asked from a bed to my right.

"The teachers are mean, too," said someone on my other side. "And we'll be sent home if we complain."

"I'd like to go home," another voice said.

"It isn't right, though. They're really mean," said a fourth voice in the dark.

I thought about how well I'd been treated at home by my father and grandparents. They never hit me when I was bad. They explained to me that what I was doing was wrong, and said that I should stop. It didn't seem right that the matrons—Indians themselves, although not Navajos—mistreated us, their fellow Indians.[8]

Yet the children persisted. It was in school that they learned to sleep in beds, live by the clock, and discipline their minds to learn and write in a new language. Some went to Catholic or Protestant parochial schools operated as missionary outreach programs. Others went to secular schools. All the schools were intolerant of Navajo society, pitting the children between wanting to learn new things and remaining within their own culture. Almost without exception the children—and then young adults—looked forward to the summer when they could return to their homes and live in quiet harmony with family, friends, and nature.

Day by day they grew toward adulthood. Just as they reached maturity, war broke out in Europe. It was then, despite all the indignities that had been heaped on the Navajo people, that their tribal council issued a proclamation that they would support the United States in war, should it come:

> Whereas, the Navajo Tribal Council and the 50,000 people we represent, cannot fail to recognize the crisis now facing the world in the threat of foreign invasion and the destruction of the great liberties and benefits which we enjoy on the reservation, and
>
> Whereas, there exists no purer concentration of Americanism than among the First Americans, and
>
> Whereas, it has become common practice to attempt national destruction through the sowing of seeds of treachery among minority groups such as ours, and
>
> Whereas, we hereby serve notice that any un-American movement among our people will be resented and dealt with severely, and
>
> Now, Therefore, we resolve that the Navajo Indians stand ready as they did in 1918, to aid and defend our Government and its institutions against all subversive and armed conflict and pledge our loyalty to the system which recognizes minority rights and a way of life that has placed us among the great people of our race.[9]

In the opening months of World War II in Europe, the Germans attempted to gain the support of the Republic of Ireland in resisting the British. In World War I, the Germans had tried to enlist Mexico against the United States and even tried to sow the seeds of dissent among minority groups in the United States to undermine national will. Political instability in an adversary is always an aim of a dictator. It was in response to these earlier efforts that the tribal council made their declaration of loyalty. There was no question that the Navajo people would support America in war and thwart efforts to turn them against the United States government.

CREATING THE CODE

After completing basic training, many Navajo enlistees were sent to Camp Pendleton, California, to learn the basics of military communications. They learned about existing communications methods, including semaphore and Morse code, as well as how to set up field communications stations. Most importantly, they studied the use of field radios. Since most of the group had grown up without electricity, electronics were an unfamiliar subject, but they were taught how to use the radios and how to repair them in the field.

Then, to their surprise, twenty-nine were asked if they would participate in a top-secret project. After swearing an oath of confidentiality, they were brought together in a room and told that they were to develop a unique code that could be used quickly and efficiently in battle. At that point in time, the Japanese had broken every American code, forcing the Marines to use the slow and cumbersome mechanical Shackle encryption system. There was concern that even this code would be broken because it relied on repeating patterns that the Japanese could, through trial and error, identify and eventually crack. Part of the urgency for developing an unbreakable code was that the United States had secretly broken Japan's primary code. This breakthrough led to the Navy's success in the Battle of Midway Island, since the Navy knew in advance where the Japanese force was sailing. But with success came suspicion—if the United States could break the Japanese codes, military planners had to assume the Japanese could break the Americans'.

Military leaders approached the Navajo because in World War I the United States had enjoyed some success using Native American languages as codes. However, once Germany worked out what had happened, they sent emissaries to many American tribes after World War I to learn their languages so they couldn't be used against the Germans in subsequent military action. But they hadn't sent emissaries to the Navajo. A World War I veteran by the name of Philip Johnson had spent time on the Navajo reservation as a child when his parents were sent there as missionaries. He learned to speak Navajo and recognized that since at the time it was a purely oral language, there was no practical way for either the Germans or the Japanese to figure out how the language worked. And even though Johnson had learned conversational Navajo, he recognized that with four different tones used to distinguish words, there were many Navajo words which even he could not distinguish between. For example, the words *medicine* and *mouth* are pronounced the same in Navajo but differentiated by tone. A person learning the language after age four is unable to hear the distinction between the two words. Because of that, he felt that the Navajo language was ideal for coding and presented his idea to commanders in the Marines and Army. The Army rejected his idea, but after a trial with some of Johnson's Navajo friends, the Marines expressed interest. And so the original twenty-nine code talkers found their way to a nondescript room at Camp Pendleton.

The group was told that the words in the code should have a logical connection to the terms they were describing, that they should use words that were highly descriptive to ease the task of memorization but also use words as short as possible to speed transmission—and that the code should feature only words that were quite different from each other to reduce confusion. The men in charge then told them they were on their own and that they shouldn't come out of the room until they had something concrete. With that, they closed and locked the door, leaving it to the twenty-nine Navajo Marines to figure out how to proceed.

At first, the young men acknowledged that none of them had any experience in creating codes. But as they talked, they began to come up with ideas. The most important was that even though they'd been given a list of more than 200 military words that should have direct counterparts in Navajo, they decided first to identify Navajo words to represent each letter in the English alphabet so they could spell out any word they were handed in case a shortcut didn't exist. To do this, they first chose an English word to represent a letter in the alphabet, such as "ant" for *A*. The Navajo equivalent of ant was *wol-a-chee*. For the letter *B* they chose "bear," which sounded like *shush* in Navajo. When all twenty-six letters were represented by an English word and the Navajo equivalent identified, they had a code that could transmit virtually any message.

But they also recognized that in the heat of battle it would be far too cumbersome and time-consuming to spell out every single English word. They needed shortcuts for words that would be used frequently—but obscure enough shortcuts that the Japanese couldn't easily look for frequency patterns in their attempts to break the code. This presented a problem. Since the twenty-nine had no military training prior to the war, they did not understand what many of the military words and phrases even meant, which made it impossible to come up with meaningful Navajo substitute words. They requested three additional already-experienced Marine Navajos to be added to their group. These three quickly became part of the group and helped identify more than 500 Navajo words to substitute directly for military terms. The original twenty-nine felt that these men should always be included as part of the founding group, so most refer to the "original thirty-two" in their memoirs rather than twenty-nine.

In identifying the direct substitutions, the thirty-two chose clever visual words. For example, airplanes were named for specific birds. The bombs the planes dropped were "eggs." Dive bombers were identified as "sparrow hawks," which dive on their prey in the wild. A fighter plane, on the other hand, was referred to using the Navajo word for hummingbird. A battleship was a whale; a navy destroyer was a shark.

As the code expanded, the coders had to spend hundreds of hours memorizing and practicing it. It's one thing to know that a battleship is a whale, but quite another to remember it under fire while translating from English to Navajo and from Navajo back to English, while making sure that there were no mistakes. Eventually, as additional Navajos were recruited into the program, a formal training program was instituted that required an additional four weeks, with 176 hours devoted to the code in addition to basic training. Beyond that, the code talkers spent hundreds of hours practicing to make sure they got it right.

While the code is the focus of this chapter, the code talkers' time spent in basic training and in combat should not be overlooked. The Navajos were trained as Marines, with all the rigorous physical conditioning and military discipline that requires. The greatest challenge was cultural, however, not physical. The Navajo men could run as far as anyone. They received exceptional scores for marksmanship with both rifles and handguns. Chester Nez wrote:

> I especially liked the rifle range. It was like a game, with everyone competing. We men took turns setting up targets and recording the results of each recruit's practice volleys.
>
> "Damn!" The instructor pored over our score

sheets. "I've never seen anything like it." He shook his head. "Where'd you guys learn to shoot?"

We felt pretty comfortable on the rifle range and with our pistols, and Platoon 382 earned one of the highest scores in marksmanship of any Marine platoon in history. We graduated with one expert, fourteen sharpshooters, and twelve marksmen in our ranks. That got us another write-up in the Marine Corps *Chevron* [the Marine Corps magazine]. I was qualified as a pistol sharpshooter.[10]

Because the code was a secret, only a handful of the regular Marines they interacted with had any idea they were part of a top-secret project. Others just assumed they were combat-ready Marines. The Navajo liked that. Keeping secrets was not a challenge. In time, they were ready to go to sea—and to find their way to the beaches of Guadalcanal in the hottest days of battle.

NAVAJOS IN BATTLE— HIGHLY RESPECTED WARRIORS

First, it should be said that all men who went into battle in the South Pacific faced mind-numbing fear, hardship, and deprivation. This was true regardless of race or background. While on ships at sea in the Pacific theater, sailors, soldiers, and Marines had to fear attack by kamikaze pilots. After landing on the beaches and then in the jungles, they lived in fear of banzai attacks by Japanese soldiers rushing forward in the middle of the night, screaming like banshees to disorient the Americans. The humidity and rain were oppressive, making it almost impossible for them to keep their feet and clothing dry; tropical diseases, including malaria, often left them weak and enervated. Many times they were cut off from supplies when Japanese aircraft drove the American support ships farther out to sea, so that hunger and thirst were an ominous reality.

The Navajo shared these challenges with all who served. They did feel better equipped to deal with hunger, since they had experienced it in their youth, but the fear and exhaustion took as great a toll on the code talkers as it did on everyone else. Beach warfare was particularly brutal. The Japanese strategy was to occupy key islands south and east of Japan from which they could launch aircraft to protect their supply lines. The primary reason Japan went to war with the United States is that we had restricted their access to natural resources because of their brutal treatment of the Chinese. The Japanese goal was to establish military dominance (hegemony) in the Pacific so that they could draw on the energy, metals, and other natural resources that they lacked in their home islands. Once the Japanese were entrenched on an island, they were fierce fighters who would prefer to fight to the death than ever to surrender. Surrendering caused lifetime shame for both those who gave in as well as their families back home.

The Americans would wage war in this situation by bombarding the beaches with ship-based artillery and aerial bombing for several days in advance of landing troops. After thousands of tons of explosives were dropped on key spots, it was easy to hope that all the Japanese had been killed before the landing, but that was never the case. The Japanese would hunker down—sometimes in caves, other times in hand-dug foxholes—and the majority would survive to assault the Marines as their landing craft approached the beaches. The Japanese always enjoyed the advantage since, by definition, they held the high ground above the water, and it's easier to fire down than up. It took brute force and many casualties to secure a beachhead from which to move inland to defeat the recalcitrant Japanese.

All these dead bodies posed a special problem for the Navajo. As one biographer explains:

> The Navajo trait that posed the most difficult
> problem for code talkers in the Pacific was the fear of

death. This did not mean that the Navajos were un-usually afraid of dying. Rather, they wanted no part of anything that had already died. The Navajo faith, like many religions, taught that people are not totally extinguished at their deaths. Unlike religions such as Christianity, however, the traditional Navajo religion did not assign the souls of the dead to an afterlife in another world. Traditional Navajos believed that only the evil part of a dead creature or person lingered on Earth. The *chindi*, as these spirits were called, returned to the place of their dying to terrorize the living. *Chindi* were to be avoided at all costs.

Because of their fear and hatred of *chindi*, Navajos deliberately avoided anything remotely connected with death. Once a person was dead, his or her name was not to be mentioned again, even if the dead person was a loved one. . . . Burial was an ominous task, with elaborate ritual precautions taken to protect those who had to perform it. The Navajos' fear of spirits of death was so powerful that many did not even like to look at the bodies of dead animals.

In the Pacific war, the Navajo code talkers were surrounded by *chindi*, more *chindi* than they could have imagined in their worst fears. They lived among death and slept among death. Bodies of dying and dead comrades had to be pulled out of slimy rivers and vine-choked ditches. Navajos on the front lines hud-dled in their foxholes all night long while dead ene-mies lay in the darkness around them.

Yet even this unsettling closeness with their worst fear did not deter the Navajo code talkers from carrying out their duties. One code talker reported: "One night a screaming Japanese soldier leaped into the trench and killed my partner with a samurai sword before other marines could shoot him. I had to stay there sending messages with my friend's blood gushing over me."

The Navajos showed a great ability to accept circumstances beyond their control. As much as they feared the *chindi*, there was no escape from the dead. Death was a fact of life in the Pacific war. Survival instincts were stronger even than the fear of all traditional taboos, and so the Navajos simply learned to live with their situation.[11]

This demonstrates just how brave and loyal the code talkers were to the United States. In their homes in the desert they would have never thought of stepping over another person, even at night, because that was a sign of disrespect. In battle, they had to accept living conditions that violated their sense of the Right Way on an almost daily basis. One of the situations that bothered them the most was going into battle from a landing craft that dropped them in the water near a beach under fire. Dead bodies floated all around them, blood staining the water. But with great courage and resolve they pushed through this death to the beach and then fought with honor until they could establish a safe position from which to start broadcasting their coded messages. Once on the beaches, they transmitted vital code, sometimes for more than twenty-four hours straight with only small breaks to take catnaps.

The code talkers always worked in pairs on both ends of the transmission. One would crank the small generator that powered the field radio's batteries while the other read handwritten messages from their field leaders and then translated them into the code to transmit to the receiving team at the command center onboard the support ships. When the code talker's voice grew hoarse from speaking, he would switch places with his partner to crank the radio and receive the messages.

But their collaboration extended further than that. Since radio transmissions can be heard by everyone tuned into that frequency, all the Navajo in a group would listen in whenever possible to make sure there were no errors in the transmission. This was a matter of life and death. For example, if a field leader sighted a Japanese unit, he gave the exact coordinates to the code talker, who then sent that information to a team assigned to an artillery group farther back. Even the slightest error in coordinates could result in artillery shells falling on friendly forces rather than the enemy.

Perhaps the most remarkable thing about the code talkers is how few errors were made. Their error rate, in fact, was so low it was statistically insignificant. As noted earlier, the most difficult battle of the war was the assault on the island of Iwo Jima, south of the Japanese homeland, near the end of the war. The Japanese were situated high up on the volcanic mountains above the landing Marines and could fire down on them at will. This was not a typical tropical island with palm trees and jungle. Rather it was a sulfuric slag heap that injured lungs and left soldiers exposed for the enemy to exploit. But in the first twenty-four hours of the American assault on Iwo Jima, the code talkers broadcast more than 800 essential messages without a single error. Having this almost instantaneous intelligence to act upon saved countless lives and assisted in an ultimate United States victory.

It is beyond the scope of this chapter to review each of the battles in which the Navajo code talkers participated, but they included Guadalcanal, Bougainville, Guam, Peleliu, Angaur, Saipan, Iwo Jima, Okinawa, and others—in other words, most of the major battles in the Pacific theater.

In these battles, the Navajo were treated with respect by those with whom they fought. Unlike the African Americans who served in World War II, the Navajo were fully integrated into regular Army and Marine units. Their Native American heritage earned them admiration and respect. Their polite demeanor and willingness to endure hardship was recognized from their very first days in battle. Only occasionally did they run into trouble because of their facial features and use of the Navajo language. Since the code was a protected secret, white American servicemen sometimes mistook the Navajo for Japanese who had stolen an American uniform. On a few occasions the Navajo were incarcerated, and at least once threatened with death, until a senior officer could intervene to protect them. Fortunately, none were ever killed by intentional friendly fire.

A touching story shows the strain they worked under when the war came to an unexpected end with the detonation of the second atomic bomb dropped on Japan:

> Okinawa fell to American forces after a bloody struggle that left the marines wary of the next leg of the journey: an invasion of the main Japanese islands. As they waited on Okinawa in August 1945 for word of what was to happen next, a Navajo working the radio received a message. Instantly he leaped to his feet and started dancing. Pounding out a rhythm as he danced, he made his way to the officers' tents. There he broke the news that, following the atomic-bomb blasts destroying Hiroshima and Nagasaki, Japan had surrendered.[12]

Imagine the relief felt by all American Marines, Navy, and Army who were relieved of the burden of invading the Japanese home islands. Still, it was a Navajo who chose to dance in joy at the news!

AFTER THE WAR

Each of the Navajos returned home when they reached the specified number of points to qualify, returning one by one to a nation that had no idea of their contributions to the war. While respected in battle, they returned home to the prejudice that had dogged them all their lives before the war. Many people thought them lazy and unwashed. It was difficult to compete with returning white soldiers for jobs and education. Chester Nez ran right into the prejudice on his return to Albuquerque, New Mexico, after being mustered out of the Marines:

> Enroute, I stopped at the federal building in Gallup, New Mexico, to get an identification card, a card that was required for Native Americans at that time. Dressed in my spotless Marine uniform, I entered the building with confidence and approached the desk of a civilian paper pusher. From behind his desk, the man stared at me, the Navajo Marine, and his eyes narrowed.
>
> "You're not a *full* citizen of the United States, you know." Wielding the small power given to him by his position, the man pressed his lips together and raised his brows in a contemptuous expression. "You can't even vote."
>
> "I'm a Marine. I'm on my way home after serving my country in battle," I said. I took a deep breath and told myself to stay calm. This guy didn't know anything. But I didn't much like what the civil servant had to say.
>
> I stared at the smug man. "I wish I had my forty-five with me," I said. I pointed my finger like a gun, aiming at the man's chest. "I'd shoot you right there. Right there." I turned around and walked out, ignoring the protests that followed me out the door.
>
> Although Native Americans were made citizens of the United States in 1924, we weren't finally granted the right to vote in New Mexico until 1948, three years after I finished my service as a Navajo code talker in the Pacific War.[13]

This is the only instance in Nez's autobiography where he expresses frustration with his cultural situation. He made it past this incident and returned to his family where he was warmly welcomed—but not celebrated, since it is expected that a Navajo will do his duty in battle. He wished desperately to share the story of the code talkers with his father, but the Marines had classified the program in case it was needed again in a future conflict.

Nez and many other Navajo were tormented in their dreams by the ferocious fighting and scenes of death. Nez felt that the *chindi* of the Japanese soldiers who had been killed by the Marines were tormenting him. His stress was likely post-traumatic stress disorder, which is better understood today than it was at the end of World War II. When the stress became unbearable, he confessed to his sister, his father, and to a village "trembler," who used Nez's hands to detect what type of Navajo purification ceremony would best help him to lay the ghosts to rest. Chester participated in an "Enemy Way" ceremony to counteract the *chindi* that troubled him. This was a three-day event in which people danced and sang around him but never touched him. The hair of a Japanese soldier was required for the ceremony to work. Fortunately, some Navajo had clipped the hair of their dead enemy and sent it home, so this essential element was present. The cost of putting on a "Sing" ceremony, as it was called, was borne by his family. It required feeding anyone who chose to attend, not just from their own village, but from anywhere. It was a sacrifice, but in his situation it brought relief. Chester's nightmares faded until later in his life.

The second type of ceremony was a "Blessing Way" ceremony to invite peace and harmony back into a person's life. The more than 400 Navajo code talkers were all beneficiaries of these ceremonies held in their behalf throughout the Navajo Nation. But the loss of prestige from their time at war took a toll on many. Some men, who were introduced to alcohol in their time in the service, fell into alcoholism. Others suffered through low-paying jobs and loss of self-respect for the rest of their lives.

In 1968, the military finally declassified the code project, and the Navajo began to receive recognition for the incredible work they had performed in the Pacific. First was a letter of appreciation to all code talkers from President Richard Nixon in 1971. In 1982, President Ronald Reagan declared August 14 as National Code Talkers Day, and in 1992 a special exhibit honoring the code talkers was dedicated at the Pentagon. In 2000, Senator Jeff Bingaman of New Mexico introduced Senate Bill 2408, the "Honoring the Navajo Code Talkers Act," which was signed into law by President Bill Clinton in December. Finally, on July 26, 2001, President George W. Bush presented Congressional Gold Medals to the surviving original code talkers in a ceremony in the Capitol building in Washington, DC. Medals were sent posthumously to the others, including Congressional Silver Medals for those who came after the original code talkers. Here are President Bush's remarks:

> Thank you very much. Today, America honors 21 Native Americans who, in a desperate hour, gave their country a service only they could give. In war, using their native language, they relayed secret messages that turned the course of battle. At home, they carried for decades the secret of their own heroism. Today, we give these exceptional Marines the recognition they earned so long ago. . . .
>
> The gentlemen with us, John Brown, Chester Nez, Lloyd Oliver, Allen Dale June and Joe Palmer, represented by his son Kermit, are the last of the original Navajo Code Talkers. In presenting gold medals to each of them, the Congress recognizes their individual service, bravely offered and flawlessly performed.
>
> With silver medals, we also honor the dozens more who served later, with the same courage and distinction. And with all these honors, America pays tribute to the tradition and community that produced

such men, the great Navajo Nation. The paintings in this rotunda tell of America and its rise as a nation. Among them are images of the first Europeans to reach the coast, and the first explorer to come upon the Mississippi.

But before all these firsts on this continent, there were the first people. They are depicted in the background, as if extras in the story. Yet, their own presence here in America predates all human record. Before others arrived, the story was theirs alone.

Today we mark a moment of shared history and shared victory. We recall a story that all Americans can celebrate, and every American should know. It is a story of ancient people, called to serve in a modern war. It is a story of one unbreakable oral code of the Second World War, messages traveling by field radio on Iwo Jima in the very language heard across the Colorado Plateau centuries ago.

Above all, it's a story of young Navajos who brought honor to their nation and victory to their country. Some of the Code Talkers were very young, like Albert Smith, who joined the Marines at 15. In order to enlist, he said, I had to advance my age a little bit. At least one code talker was over-age, so he claimed to be younger in order to serve. On active duty, their value was so great, and their order so sensitive, that they were closely guarded. By war's end, some 400 Navajos had served as Code Talkers. Thirteen were killed in action, and their names, too, are on today's roll of honor.

Regardless of circumstances, regardless of history, they came forward to serve America. The Navajo code itself provides a part of the reason. Late in his life, Albert Smith explained, the code word for America was, "Our Mother." Our Mother stood for freedom, our religion, our ways of life, and that's why we went in. The Code Talkers joined 44,000 Native Americans who wore the uniform in World War II. More than 12,000 Native Americans fought in World War I. Thousands more served in Korea, Vietnam and serve to this very day.

Twenty-four Native Americans have earned the highest military distinction of all, the Medal of Honor, including Ernest Childers, who was my guest at the White House last week. In all these wars and conflicts, Native Americans have served with the modesty and strength and quiet valor their tradition has always inspired.

That tradition found full expression in the Code Talkers, in those absent, and in those with us today. Gentlemen, your service inspires the respect and admiration of all Americans, and our gratitude is expressed for all time, in the medals it is now my honor to present.

May God bless you all.[14]

An eloquent tribute to highly deserving men. It brought balance to their service and sacrifice, putting them in tune with the Right Way of living.

CHAPTER 7

THE PURPLE HEART BATTALION
RESCUING THE TEXAS 1ST

osges Mountains, France, October 30, 1944: As many as seven
hundred well-supplied German soldiers surrounded the 211 surviving members of the 1st Battalion of the Texas 141st Regiment[1]
and were biding their time for the Americans to surrender. Six days
previously, the 1st Battalion had been cut off from their own lines,
and in that time the Americans had run out of food and fuel. Even
worse, they'd lost sixty-four of their comrades to the Germans. The
soldiers of the 1st Battalion had done a remarkable job of keeping
the Germans at bay, given the ratio of enemy to friend, but their
time was almost up. They were desperate and cold with, they feared,
no rescue in sight.

In a war where the Allies had consistently pushed the Germans
back since the British victory at El Alamein in North Africa, this
was finally a chance for the Germans to take some prisoners of
their own. So important were the propaganda opportunities of this

encirclement that Adolf Hitler intervened to order his field commanders to prevent the escape of the 1st Battalion, regardless of German losses.[2] With that kind of resistance massed against them, nothing short of a miracle could save the Americans.

That miracle was about to show up in an unexpected way. Despite heavy fighting and losses farther south, a battle-hardened battalion from Hawaii was ordered back into the fray after just two days' rest. Their objective was to rescue the 1st Battalion. On its way, this new group would suffer hundreds of casualties to rescue the 211 men of the Texas 1st Battalion. It was a high-stakes conflict amid the greatest conflict in human history.

FIGHTING THROUGH ITALY INTO FRANCE

The 1st Battalion found itself in this predicament as the result of a six-mile thrust into enemy territory on October 24, 1944. A companion group, the 3d Battalion, advanced parallel to their line until a German counterattack separated the two groups. With overwhelming numbers, the Germans encircled the 1st Battalion and confined them to a narrow ridge toward the top of a heavily wooded mountain. Only three things could happen to the Texans: the battalion would break out and make their way back to friendly lines; they would be killed; or they'd be taken as prisoners.

On the first night of encirclement, they decided to try for a limited breakout. Under cover of darkness, they sent a party of thirty-six of their best men out to sneak through enemy lines to bring back food and supplies from friendly forces. What they didn't know is that the American Fifth Army line had contracted, and the 1st was now nine miles behind enemy lines. Shortly after sneaking out of camp, the group ran into a nest of Germans. In the firefight that followed, thirty-one of thirty-six were killed, and the five survivors retreated with wounds back to the main group on top of the mountain. The war of attrition was on.

After that, the Germans made daily thrusting movements against the Americans to draw their fire, using up valuable ammunition. They also deployed a tank each day to move forward against the 1st, forcing the Americans to fight back with active fire and ammunition so the Germans couldn't get a good estimate of just how fragile their situation was. But with each American bullet expended, their options diminished. The Germans, who now held a decisive advantage on all sides, had no need to risk a major attack; once the Americans' ammunition ran out, it was over.

Fortunately, the battle-fatigued men of the 100th Hawaiian Infantry, now joined by members of the Texas 442nd Regimental Combat Team (the 100th/442nd RCT), were fighting their way to the rescue, with progress sometimes measured in just a few feet of soil gained. What made the 100th/442nd RCT unique is that it was the only unit in the US Army made up almost exclusively of *Nisei* (second-generation Japanese American) soldiers, whose valor throughout the war would make them the most highly decorated unit of World War II. This included several hundred Purple Hearts and twenty-one Medals of Honor[3] (the highest military award bestowed by the United States for valor above and beyond the call of duty). In this and other campaigns, the Nisei proved both their loyalty and their bravery with deeds of heroism that contradicted what many back home in the United States thought of their fellow—and frequently disparaged—Japanese American citizens.

THE PURPLE HEART BATTALION

The Purple Heart Battalion, named for the staggering number of casualties its members suffered in combat, was made up of two groups of Japanese-descended Americans. The first was the 100th Battalion formed by loyal Japanese American young men from Hawaii, of which most were former members of the Hawaii National Guard. The second, the 442nd, consisted of nearly 3,000

Japanese Americans from Hawaii and 1,500 young men whose families were part of the relocation program enforced against Japanese Americans living on the West Coast of the United States.[4] All were subject to racial prejudice from other citizens as they traveled within the United States and by other soldiers as they fought and died in Italy and France, yet they served valiantly. The story of these storied combat units started immediately after Japan attacked the United States on December 7, 1941.

INSTITUTIONALIZED RACISM

The Japanese attack on Pearl Harbor on the Hawaiian island of Oahu created frantic anti-Japanese hysteria on the West Coast of the United States, with rumors of pending Japanese attacks on California, Oregon, and Washington. Logistically this was almost impossible, since Japan lacked the ability to deploy a naval force that far from home, particularly after the destruction of most Japanese aircraft carriers in the Battle of Midway six months after Pearl Harbor.

Still, a small group of officials in Washington, DC, and on the West Coast responded to the public's fear of a Japanese "fifth column" of saboteurs among the many Japanese American citizens living there. It was easy to racially profile Japanese immigrants (*Issei*) and their American-born sons and daughters (*Nisei*), because of their physical appearance. Within days of the attack on Pearl Harbor, Japanese Americans serving in the armed forces were stripped of their weapons and discharged from service. Despite virtually no evidence of disloyalty by Japanese Americans, President Franklin D. Roosevelt issued the now-infamous Executive Order 9066 on February 19, 1942, which authorized the relocation and internment of more than 120,000 people of Japanese descent into ten guarded camps deep in the United States' interior. Essentially, all people of Japanese descent on the mainland were forbidden to live or operate in the three western coastal states, as well as parts of western Arizona.[5]

With this order, entire families were sent to one of ten concentration camps in the interior without due process or even suspicion of wrongdoing. In many cases, they had to sell their homes and businesses at discounts approaching 80 to 90 percent of prewar market value because of the hurried time frame of the evacuation.

Was this necessary? With respect to German and Italian Americans (whose native countries were also at war with the United States), only 15,000 who were investigated for their membership in anti-American organizations—or who were considered dangerous—were incarcerated during the war. In contrast, more than 95 percent of Americans of Japanese ancestry were sent to concentration camps; fewer than half of 1 percent of those of German and Italian ancestry were detained. A 1980 presidential commission on wartime relocation and internment examined all aspects of the program and concluded that it had little basis in security but was based on racial prejudice.[6] Consider this quote from Lieutenant General John L. DeWitt, who ultimately administered the relocation program:

> I don't want any of them here. They are a dangerous element. There is no way to determine their loyalty. The West Coast contains too many vital installations essential to the defense of the country to allow any Japanese on this coast. . . . The danger of the Japanese was, and is now—if they are permitted to come back—espionage and sabotage. It makes no difference whether he is an American citizen, he is still a Japanese. American citizenship does not necessarily determine loyalty. . . . But we must worry about the Japanese all the time until he is wiped off the map. Sabotage and espionage will make problems as long as he is allowed in this area.[7]

The program did not have unanimous support. In fact, J. Edgar Hoover, director of the FBI, found no basis for mass incarceration. Nor did the military governor of Hawaii, where nearly 40 percent of the population were of Japanese descent (compared to just 5 percent on the West Coast). The citizens of Hawaii had far greater experience with their Japanese neighbors, working alongside them in business and in their neighborhoods. The Hawaiian military leaders took the more sensible course of rounding up just the handful that might pose a threat and incarcerating them after a fair investigation.

It was also in Hawaii that the Purple Heart Battalion was born. On May 26, 1942, Lieutenant General Delos C. Emmons received permission from General George C. Marshall to form the Hawaiian Provisional Battalion, later christened the 100th Infantry Battalion. To prevent confusion in the field, the 1,432 men of the 100th were to be deployed to the European theater of action rather than the Pacific after training in Wisconsin and Mississippi. From training, they went to Oran, Algeria, where they prepared for the invasion of Italy. The war began in earnest for the Nisei with their landing in Salerno, Italy, in September 1943. Nine months later, after fierce combat, the battalion was down to just 521 members—a loss of more than 900 dead and wounded. On June 10, 1944, the Hawaiian Battalion (100th Infantry Battalion) was combined with the Nisei from the 442nd Regimental Combat Team in Anzio, Italy. In September 1944, the unit was sent to France, where they would, just weeks later, rescue the stranded 1st Battalion high in the Vosges Mountains.[8]

While anti-Japanese sentiment continued unabated in the United States, the incredibly brave men of the 442nd smashed racial boundaries in Italy and later in France. Many GIs serving in the Fifth Army quickly recognized the competence and bravery of their diminutive companions from Hawaii and the West Coast. Many recalled later that in the fight with the Germans, they always felt more at ease knowing that the 100th/442nd had their backs.

THE LOST BATTALION IS FOUND

After being called up to rescue their comrades, it took five days for the 100th/442nd to drive a wedge through German lines to reach the hilltop where the 1st Battalion was encamped. On the way, they encountered minefields and roadblocks. Holding the high ground provided a distinct advantage for the Germans, who rained small arms fire and artillery down on the advancing Americans. One hill was so costly to take that it was nicknamed Suicide Hill. One account of the October 29, 1944, assault on Suicide Hill is by C. Douglas Sterner, based on interviews of members of the 110th/442nd included in his book, *Go for Broke*:

> Second Lieutenant Edward Davis was the only officer left in company K. Slowly he rose to his feet as the Nisei around him watched in amazement. All knew the order to assault the enemy above them would be suicidal and were reluctant to move further. The lieutenant turned to Sergeant Kohashi and asked, not ordered, the NCO to follow him. Then something amazing happened. Sergeant Kohashi rose to his feet with a loud yell of desperation that reverberated across the hillside. It shook the Japanese-American soldiers to the soul, eliciting similar cries. As a unit, the Nisei leaped to their feet screaming "banzai" as they charged the Germans.
>
> In his own sector, Private Barney Hajiro rose to his feet to lead his own assault. Next to him was a friend he had known since basic training, Takeyasu "Thomas" Onaga. As they moved forward young Hajiro watched in horror as the close friend who moments earlier had loaded his Browning automatic rifle, fell dead to a hail of enemy bullets. . . . With abandon he assaulted "suicide hill," yards ahead of the other men of his platoon. . . . Private Barney Hajiro quickly knocked out two

enemy gun emplacements and shot two snipers, allowing the rest of his unit to advance. Then enemy rounds slammed into Private Hajiro's left arm, rendering it useless.

The banzai charge on "suicide hill" consumed an hour. The Nisei suffered many casualties, but by 15:30 they had taken the hill. Those enemy soldiers who were wounded or otherwise unable to escape the hill cowered in fear before the survivors of the onslaught. Never had they seen such courage, such fierce determination, and such sheer force of will power in the face of unbelievable odds.[9]

The following day, October 30, two units of Nisei pressed forward through heavy enemy resistance. At one point the Germans outnumbered the Nisei four to one. Yet the Nisei prevailed, breaking through to the beleaguered Americans of the 1st Battalion in mid-afternoon. Private First Class Matsuji "Mutt" Sakumoto, the first American soldier to break through, casually said to the startled men, "You guys need cigarettes?" as if nothing much had happened.[10] One of the rescued men, Major Claude D. Roscoe, later said, "To our great pleasure it was members of the 442nd Combat Team. We were overjoyed to see these people for we knew them as the best fighting men in the ETO (European Theater of Operations)."[11]

LEGACY

During twenty-six days in October and November 1944—including the campaign to rescue the Lost Battalion—the Nisei of the 100th/442nd suffered nearly 2,000 casualties—140 killed and 1,800 wounded.[12] Virtually every soldier of the Nisei who survived earned the Purple Heart for being wounded in combat.

A touching story added to virtually every account of this battle describes the men of the 100th/442nd being called to assembly by

Major General John Dahlquist two weeks after the rescue of the Lost Battalion. The general was piqued when so few men assembled, thinking that some were snubbing his order. When he asked about it, the reply was that all surviving members of the unit were turned out—the small number was due to the casualties they had suffered in the previous weeks.[13]

In the months that followed, the Purple Heart Battalion received the Presidential Unit Citation and sixteen Division Citations. Five Nisei who fought in the Vosges Mountains, including Private Hajiro who led the banzai assault on Suicide Hill, later received the Medal of Honor.

As for the Japanese American internment camps, it became clear to Americans even during the war that there was no justified cause for the imprisonment. Two Supreme Court decisions in late 1944 declared that removal in war was justified, but internment of loyal citizens was not. In January 1945, the camps opened their gates to allow the illegally imprisoned Americans to return home.

Perhaps the greatest proof of their loyalty is that in the annals of World War II not a single case of espionage against an American of Japanese descent was ever filed, let alone prosecuted.

On August 10, 1988, President Ronald Reagan signed the Civil Liberties Act of 1988, which acknowledged the injustice of incarcerating loyal Americans for no other reason than their racial heritage. It provided approximately $20,000 compensation to each surviving detainee at a total cost of $1.6 billion. That was a small fraction of the financial losses suffered in 1942, but it provided a formal acknowledgment of their innocence and loyalty. On December 7, 1991, while speaking at a Pearl Harbor memorial service in Hawaii, President George H. W. Bush issued a formal apology on behalf of the United States:

> In remembering, it is important to come to grips
> with the past. No nation can fully understand itself

or find its place in the world if it does not look with clear eyes at all the glories and disgraces, too, of the past. We in the United States acknowledge such an injustice in our history: The internment of Americans of Japanese ancestry was a great injustice, and it will never be repeated.[14]

Through their valor in battle and their integrity in war, the Japanese-descended Americans who fought in behalf of their country in World War II, the Purple Heart Battalion, not only served the cause of war, but contributed to the reduction of prejudice in the peace that followed.

CHAPTER 8

COMBAT ENGINEERS

BUILDERS AND SOLDIERS

In 1949, the city of Bonn, Germany, celebrated the opening of a new bridge across the Rhine River to replace an earlier bridge that had been destroyed by the Nazis as they retreated from France. It had taken three years to complete this bridge. Four years earlier, in March 1945, US Army combat engineers built a pontoon bridge across the same spot in exactly ten hours and sixteen minutes.[1]

Military history tends to focus on combat troops, since they are the ones to directly engage the enemy in battle. But behind each frontline trooper stand approximately seven others who prepare the way for their military engagement. Those at greatest hazard are the combat engineers who build and repair the infrastructure necessary for the troops to move forward. Combat engineers are often right at the front line, clearing debris from roads, sweeping for mines, removing enemy-built barricades, and building or replacing bridges across everything from small creeks to mighty rivers.

In most instances, they do this under heavy enemy fire from both infantry (small arms) and artillery. When constructing the Rhine River bridges, combat engineers were also attacked by the German Luftwaffe (air force) who desperately wanted to stop the Allied advance at the last natural barrier between France and the German homeland. The Germans even launched their incredibly powerful V-2 rockets against the bridge builders. But the combat engineers persisted until numerous bridges at key points were placed for the Allied armies to advance.

The story of combat engineers is one of heroism and ingenuity under fire, as well as accomplishments that often seem miraculous for their ability to respond to changing battlefield conditions. They are the invisible soldiers who make victory possible.

THE ROLE OF COMBAT ENGINEERS

Engineers are the people who have to make things work in the real world. In combat, their roles generally fall into three types of activities: (1) defensive measures to protect against an advancing enemy; (2) offensive measures when their own troops are moving forward; and (3) rehabilitation and repair after a battle is ended. A typical combat engineering group during WWII was led by professionally trained engineers, with non-engineers doing the physical work and learning the practical side of engineering.

Consider the role of bridges. When a military unit is advancing, it encounters countless obstacles, including ravines and gullies, small streams and rivers, and even highway overpasses that require bridges across land. In an advance, bridges are an asset. But when the unit is retreating, the commanders don't want those bridges to be available to the pursuing enemy, so the orders are to destroy as many as possible to slow down the enemy's advance.

In World War II, the battlefront changed often as one side or the other gained an advantage. When the Allies were in retreat, their engineers helped the combat troops by creating obstacles to the enemy's advance. One technique was to build an abatis, which involved felling trees across roadways in such a fashion that their roots and branches interlocked. Time was always limited, so dynamite often supplemented saws in bringing down large trees. Precious time was gained for the Allied infantry when the Germans had to stop to clear the debris. This fortification was often supplemented with barbed wire along the sides of the roads to constrict the available lane of traffic.

It was also up to the engineers to prepare dams and bridges for destruction by placing explosive charges in critical spots. Once all the friendly troops were on the correct side of the large infrastructure, the charges were detonated to the enemy's detriment.

Engineers were also tasked with laying down mines and booby traps, during both an advance and a retreat. A well-laid minefield made it difficult for German troops to sneak up on an Allied encampment in the night. Minefields held relatively large explosive charges that could disable trucks and combat tanks, as well as maim or kill any infantry who happened to stumble into the field. Booby traps were more insidious—designed to injure and disable enemy soldiers, since it takes up more resources to rescue and aid a wounded man than a dead one. The job of laying these explosive devices and of removing them is among the most hazardous in the field, and it was the engineers who used metal detectors and other mine-detection devices to clear the roads and fields in advance of the infantry.

When it came to offensive measures, the list of tasks was even greater. For example, in the heavily wooded forests of Belgium, France, and Germany, dirt roads often became muddy bogs in the snow and rain. The engineers were tasked with keeping the roads passable. Sometimes that meant using bulldozers to place gravel and fill, including bricks and debris from bombed-out buildings. On other occasions they had to build "corduroy" roads, which entailed cutting trees and laying them perpendicular to the roadway so that Allied vehicles could drive across the trees to make it through the mud. They also used their bulldozers to clear roadways of intentional roadblocks. A favorite German fortification technique was to build wooden barricades that narrowed roads to just one lane, and then fill them with sand and bricks. Because they were too heavy for foot soldiers or light vehicles to move, the Allied engineers would use heavy construction equipment to shove them aside.

It's important to note that in most instances in the European theater, all heavy equipment had to be brought by ship from England and then moved forward to the front lines. It was even worse for the engineers in the Pacific theater, as they were thousands of miles away from their home bases, with virtually everything moving on ships.

Engineers were also responsible for operating assault boats for river crossings before a temporary bridge was in place, often operating ferry service for both troops and equipment.

Finally, it fell to the engineers to construct necessary buildings, including officer headquarters, rest and recreation centers, and ammunition dumps. This wasn't as hard in Europe as it was in the Pacific, since in Europe they could commandeer homes and public buildings. In the Pacific theater there often were no homes or public buildings, so everything had to be carried in by the US Navy.

And of course, there were the bridges—literally thousands of bridges that had to be built or rehabilitated for the Army to move forward. The innovation of the Bailey bridge, developed by the British, allowed combat engineers to do astonishing things. For example, one battalion of US combat engineers, the 291st, replaced fourteen German autobahn bridges in forty-eight hours![2] The Bailey bridge deserves further detail, as does the incredible accomplishment of crossing the Rhine.

Finally, combat engineers had to be ready to step forward at any time and take up arms in actual combat if the situation demanded it. Not only did they work under fire, but they also had to be ready to return fire at all times.

THE BAILEY BRIDGE

Donald Bailey enjoyed making model bridges as a hobby. He was a civil servant in the British War Office who realized that combat engineers needed an easy-to-assemble bridge that could be mass-produced in sections light enough to transport by military trucks and to be moved into place without cranes or other machinery. That was a tall task, given that the bridges also had to support the weight of combat tanks—between thirty and forty-five tons each!

Bailey hit on a design using lightweight steel alloys that he took to his superiors for further review. Eventually, they selected a flat truss design that became the standard for the British, Canadian, and American armies.

A truss is a kind of beam in which some elements are in compression, others in tension. A simple truss is formed by two chords (long beams) that are joined by angled pieces that form interlocking triangles. When a load imposes stress on a flat truss, the upper chord compresses against itself while the bottom chord stretches in tension. The angles between the two chords transfer stress to counteract the compression and tension. Compared to solid beams, a truss is extremely strong relative to its weight.

The Bailey bridge, which is still used today, uses prefabricated truss sections pieced together in the field. The outside vertical panels bear the weight of the bridge and resemble side rails. These are joined to cross-members that form the roadbed, which is first covered with wood and then steel if armored vehicles are to pass over. For added strength, two panels may be added to each side, up to three panels high. Using this prefabricated, easy-assembly pattern, combat engineers may build a bridge up to 200 feet long capable of carrying heavy artillery and tanks. Pedestrian walkways are sometimes added outside the vertical panels to allow troops to cross alongside vehicles.

While the completed bridge is quite elaborate, each component of the bridge is relatively simple and lightweight, each side panel weighing 570 pounds, a load that can be carried by a group of six men. The key to success is precise manufacturing of each piece so that they all fit together perfectly in the field.

Another advantage of the Bailey bridge is that by using a roller assembly, it can be cantilevered out from one side of the gap to be bridged. The fully completed assembly rolls out from the occupied side and then drops into place on top of the opposite embankment.[3]

All of this makes for an extremely versatile bridge for crossing everything from small ravines to one of the largest rivers in the world when floated on pontoons. The Bailey bridge was an invaluable tool in the combat engineer's toolkit for helping troops advance as quickly as their military success allowed.

BRIDGING THE RHINE AT REMAGEN

After the Allied landings in Normandy on D-Day, rapid advances were made through France toward Belgium and Germany. While it was demoralizing to the Germans to lose ground captured in the early days of the war, it also meant that German lines further back were condensing and growing stronger. Plus, it was one thing for German soldiers to defend ground which held no personal connection and quite another to have the Allies threatening to invade the German homeland. Accordingly, as they retreated before the Allies, German troops created as much mischief as possible to slow the Allied advance. Removing the roadblocks and replacing destroyed bridges fell to the engineers.

The biggest obstacle of all was the mighty Rhine River that forms a portion of the border between France and Germany along part of the river's 820-mile length.[4] The Rhine headwaters are high in the Swiss Alps, and it flows northward toward the Netherlands. At the city of Bonn, Germany, on the Middle Rhine (*Mittelrhein* in German), the river is approximately 1,800 feet across, flowing at the rate of seven miles per hour.

As the Allied troops advanced toward the German cities of Cologne, Bonn, and Remagen in early March 1945, they expected to find all permanent bridges destroyed. To their surprise, the mighty Ludendorff steel bridge—built in Remagen during World War I—was still standing. More than twenty other bridges had been destroyed. Recognizing the huge strategic advantage they'd realize in capturing the Ludendorff Bridge, Allied troops pressed forward immediately, overwhelming the defenders on the west bank. But as the advance guard made it approximately two-thirds of the way across, Germans on the east bank tried to blow up the bridge. Fortunately, only a small charge went off. The remaining charges placed along the length of the bridge failed to go off because Hitler had delayed giving permission to destroy the bridge for so long that German troops had to rely on a secondary fuse. In little time, the engineers patched up the hole from the small explosion, and troops and equipment started moving across the steel bridge. The German High Command recognized the danger and started a frantic effort to destroy the bridge through air and artillery attacks. All the pounding took a toll on the bridge, making it clear that it would not stand for long. Another bridge would need to be constructed.

That's where Lieutenant Colonel David Pergrin and the 291st Engineer Combat Battalion came to the scene. Pergrin and the

291st were tasked with building a treadway (or pontoon) bridge across the Rhine as quickly as possible to facilitate movement of tanks and other armored vehicles, with pedestrian walkways on the outer edges for infantry. Pontoons float on the water, with the bridge superstructure connecting the pontoons to each other and to the riverbank. Combat conditions required that they work under almost constant bombardment from German artillery situated on the bluffs high above the east bank. But, with a heroic record of achievement and experience, they accepted the task on March 7, 1945, and set to work immediately.

The list of equipment needed to build a treadway bridge is impressive. Standard six-by-six trucks, a compressor truck, a specially designed crane that moved out onto the river as the bridge inched its way forward, and dump trucks and bulldozers to prepare the approaches to the bridge on each side of the river.

The pontoons were made of rubberized canvas tubing and were thirty-three feet long, eight feet wide, and thirty-three inches deep. Each pontoon weighed 1,000 pounds and could support eighteen tons of steel deck and live load (the vehicles and men passing over the bridge).[5] Like the Bailey bridge, each steel section was interchangeable with another, and all components essentially snapped together with connecting pins. It was a marvel of prefabricated engineering designed for speed and ease of installation.

While many of these bridges had been used to quickly cross smaller streams, none had ever been built on a river the width of the Rhine. The engineering challenges were daunting. For example, the farther the bridge extended into the river, the more the river's current interfered with the proper alignment of the bridge, which made it extremely difficult to pound the connecting pins into place. This problem was solved, in part, by using kedge anchors weighing 100 pounds each, which were dropped above the bridge in the stream and would fix themselves to the bottom of the riverbed to resist the current pulling against the bridge. Once all the sections were in place, an extremely strong one-and-a-half-inch-thick steel cable would be stretched from shore to shore to supplement the anchors; but while the bridge was under construction, there was a constant struggle to maintain alignment.[6]

The Germans also created problems with constant attacks on the bridge. In the end, the engineers had to requisition more than twice as many pontoons as were called for, as the pontoons were being ripped apart by shrapnel on a near-regular schedule. By the end of the first day, the leading edge of the bridge had been dubbed Suicide Point by the engineers working midstream.[7]

Here is one of many examples that demonstrate how enemy fire made the engineers' work both deadly and challenging:

> From [nine P.M.] March 9, until midnight, the German artillery zeroed in on the bridges, particularly our treadway bridge. This marked the beginning of the midnight counteract by the 9th and 11th SS Panzer divisions Colonel Bill Carter had forecasted. At the stroke of midnight, the night skies were lit up by the heavy artillery fire put out by both sides, and we all were forced to halt work and take cover. . . .
>
> Direct hits struck the bridge and construction sites. Equipment was set ablaze and exploding fuel tanks marked a certain disaster where the men had been assembling treadway floats. The bridge itself was hopping up and down like a jackrabbit as pressurized pontoons were pierced by shell fragments.
>
> There was nothing we could do. We would be powerless to act until the artillery attack let up.[8]

In spite of the hazard, the engineers kept at it, hour after hour, even in daylight, when the risk from aerial bombardment was greatest. This included runs by brand-new Luftwaffe small jet aircraft, something no one on the American side of the battle line had seen before. In one instance after a breathtaking attack by jet fighters, the ground on the Allied side of the river shook with the largest concussion anyone had experienced in the war, caused by V-2 rockets launched indiscriminately toward the bridges. Because the V-2s were not guided missiles, they caused no direct damage to any of the bridges, but the shaking of the ground added to the stress on the already weakened Ludendorff Bridge.

A noon attack on the second day of construction destroyed thirteen pontoons, which meant they had to be painstakingly removed from under the steel treadway and replaced with new floats. While the outcome of the project is now settled, it was not at all certain to the men fighting the battle at the time. Until the Germans on the opposite bank could be cleared from the bluff, they had almost perfect sight lines for their artillery, and until the three pontoon bridges in progress were complete, it was impossible to tell if enough Americans could make it to the eastern side to repulse the German counterattack.

But in time, the infantry was successful in pushing the Germans back from the bridgehead, expanding their circle of control. Enemy artillery became less frequent and less accurate, and work on the bridge picked up. Eventually, a bulldozer inched its way across the bridge, dragging the heavy steel cable, which was threaded through the upstream side of the treadways at strategic points. Once it reached the other side, four hours later, it was secured and tightened, bringing the bridge into perfect alignment across the river. At 7 P.M. on March 10, 1945, the bridge was finished and armored vehicles started across immediately.[9] Colonel Pergrin later wrote:

> I thought of our Remagen treadway as being a toll
> bridge, for it had taken the heaviest toll of casualties
> the battalion had yet suffered in a single place—one
> dead and thirty wounded so far. We had also had

destroyed three Quickway cranes, two Broadway trucks, two air compressors, three two-and-a-half-ton dump trucks, thirty-two floats, and considerable miscellaneous equipment and materials. The units directly supporting us had sustained additional losses.[10]

A heavy toll, indeed. And the bridge was finished none too soon. On March 11, the heavy pontoon bridge upstream from the treadway bridge opened as well. Once traffic started across these two new bridges, the massive Ludendorff was closed for badly needed repairs to the superstructure. Of course, the danger wasn't over—the Germans continued to attack the two new bridges from the air and with less discriminate artillery. Another danger also presented itself when Adolf Hitler ordered munitions experts to swim to the bridges to place explosive charges. This was prevented by three massive nets the Americans had placed upstream from their hard-won bridges—the first to snare any boats or large debris that could damage the pontoon bridges, the second to detonate any mines that the Germans tried to float downstream, and the third to ensnare swimmers. On their third attempt at sabotage, the German swimmers were spotted from shore. Immediately, powerful spotlights shone on them in the water. They made their way to the side and were taken prisoner.

At 3 P.M., March 17, ten days after the initial Allied attack on the Ludendorff Bridge, engineers were high up in the trusses welding reinforcements to stabilize the damaged bridge:

> The colonel and I were still on the treadway bridge when our attention was arrested by a loud, painful groaning from just to our south. As I instinctively glanced toward the source of the noise, I heard an even louder sound of simultaneous screeching, cracking, and splintering as steel rubbed against steel and wood. There, directly in front of me, the tired old

Ludendorff Bridge was at last giving way. As the effects of the self-demolition progressed, the immense structure swayed and then caved in. It was like watching a slow-motion movie, the progressive action was so distinct. The collapse of the Ludendorff Bridge set all available hands in the 291st to instant, instinctive rescue efforts and a frantic race to save our own span. Automatically, as soon as the big railroad bridge sounded its own death knell, my veteran engineers recovered from the shock and got to doing all the things that seemed to need doing. In no time at all, all sorts of heavy debris was floating swiftly in the current toward our vulnerable treadway floats. As the infantrymen on the treadway span speeded up their pace from route march to every man for himself, my magnificent engineers appeared as if out of nowhere with cranes, power-boats, and other equipment that could be used to rescue swimmers and prevent fatal collisions between the debris and the floats. Scores of my men ran out from either bank armed with pikes, poles, or anything that came to hand that could be used to hold off debris and direct it between the pontoons. Max Schmidt and several others drove Quickway cranes out onto the bridge in order to lift the larger, heavier pieces of planking up and over our span. As efforts to save our bridge coalesced, many of my men worked their way out onto the saddles to help pull their comrades from the largely bilged 276th Engineers out of the dangerous current.[11]

It had taken ten days for the Germans to bring down their own bridge, but it was too late. With three pontoon bridges already and more to follow, the Rhine was no longer a barrier to the Allied invasion of the German homeland. It simply wouldn't have happened without the courage and ingenuity of the combat engineers.

THE SOUTH PACIFIC

War is terrible wherever it is fought. In the European theater, engineers seldom had to take up arms directly; rather, they were protected by American infantry and artillery while they carried out their essential duties. In the South Pacific the story was very different. Landing on beaches under heavy enemy fire, the engineers fought alongside their infantry counterparts until a beachhead was established. Then they moved in with bulldozers and construction equipment to start building the necessary infrastructure to support the troops as they leapfrogged from one island to another, closing in on the main islands held by Japan.

They were up against an enemy unlike few others in history. During the capture of Okinawa, more than 150,000 natives (out of 300,000) were killed, most by the Japanese who used them as fodder at the front of their lines. 14,009 American soldiers lost their lives in the assault; 110,000 Japanese military perished. It was a bloodbath.[12]

Yet, just as soon as the fighting ended, the engineers immediately went to work rehabilitating eight damaged air bases captured from the Japanese. They also created an advanced fleet base from scratch, enlarged the naval port of Nada, and rehabilitated island roads and bridges in preparation for the expected invasion of the Japanese home islands. In addition to the threat of banzai and kamikaze attacks, the Americans were under constant threat of jungle diseases, including malaria, jungle fever, and jungle rot. Yet the engineers did their duty.

SUMMARY

While the engineers themselves seem largely invisible to history, the results of their work are not. Travel to the islands of the Pacific today, and your airplane is very likely to land on what was once an airfield originally constructed by American combat engineers. While the temporary structures of the European theater have long been replaced by permanent infrastructure, it was the Americans after the war who helped jump-start the reconstruction effort.

What happens to the engineers during peacetime? In the United States, the Army Corps of Engineers have constructed and maintain numerous dams and flood-control projects. These military warriors put their skills to work in behalf of the country itself when they are not needed overseas. Even so, today they are in Iraq, Afghanistan, Germany, South Korea, and all the other places where American troops are in harm's way. Theirs is a service and heritage of honor under fire.

CHAPTER 9

AFRICAN AMERICANS AT WAR

HEROES DESPITE PREJUDICE

African Americans have served in the United States military since the Revolutionary War. Five thousand served with distinction in the Continental Army, while 20,000 served on the side of the British, many motivated by the fact that the British promised American slaves their freedom if they escaped to British lines.[1]

Approximately 199,000 African Americans—179,000 in the Army and 20,000 in the Navy—fought with the Union in the Civil War, almost always in segregated units led by white officers.[2] Going into combat against Confederate forces held special peril for African Americans, who risked capture, ill treatment, and subsequent enslavement. One of the best known African American units in the Civil War was the 54th Massachusetts Regiment of Infantry. Recruited from among the freemen of the North, this unit served without pay for eighteen months in protest of the discriminatory practice of paying African American soldiers $7 per month ($10, with $3 withheld for clothing) instead of the $13 per month (with nothing withheld for clothing) their white counterparts received. This was despite the demands in combat being equal for both black and white men. Eventually, negative public opinion pressured Congress to correct the inequity and equalize the pay of all military personnel, regardless of race, with full compensation for the previous eighteen months.

After the Civil War, the government recognized the need for a permanent standing army to maintain order, particularly in the West. The enabling legislation created ten regiments of cavalry and forty-five regiments of infantry, including two black cavalry regiments and four black infantry regiments. Two years later, the number of infantry regiments was reduced. The four remaining African American regiments were the 9th and 10th Cavalries and the 24th and 25th Infantries. These units served with distinction in the Indian Wars and the Spanish-American War. It was during their service in the Indian Wars that African American soldiers became known as the Buffalo Soldiers, a term given them by the Native Americans. One story holds that the Cheyenne gave this name to the all-black units in 1877 because of their thick curly hair, which reminded the Native American warriors of bison fur. Another story suggests that it was bestowed in honor of the heroic fight put up by Private John Randall of Troop G of 10th Cavalry Regiment in 1867:

> Some historians contend that the nickname was a result of a specific encounter between black cavalrymen and Cheyenne Indians in Kansas. In September 1867, Private John Randall of Troop G, 10th Cavalry, was assigned to escort 2 civilians on a hunting trip. Soon after losing sight of the camp, the hunters suddenly became the hunted when a band of 70 Cheyenne warriors swept down on them. The 2 civilians quickly fell in the initial attack and Randall's horse was shot

out from beneath him. Randall managed to scramble to safety behind a washout under the railroad tracks, where he fended off the attack with only his pistol until help from the nearby camp arrived. The Indians beat a hasty retreat, leaving behind 13 fallen warriors. Private Randall suffered a gunshot wound to his shoulder and 11 lance wounds, but recovered. The Cheyenne quickly spread word of this new type of soldier, "who had fought like a cornered buffalo; who like a buffalo had suffered wound after wound, yet had not died; and who like a buffalo had a thick and shaggy mane of hair" . . . . Over time, the nickname came to apply to all black soldiers and the 10th Cavalry later incorporated the buffalo into its regimental crest.[3]

Regardless of the reason, African American soldiers of the four regiments accepted the name Buffalo Soldiers as a badge of honor and fought under that name until segregated units were disbanded by President Harry S. Truman's July 26, 1948, Executive Order to desegregate the Armed Forces.[4]

PREJUDICE

Throughout their years of service both before and after the desegregation order, black soldiers and sailors faced discrimination on and off the battlefield. During the Cuba Campaign of the Spanish-American War in 1898, the Buffalo Soldiers were treated with particular disdain. When they arrived in Tampa, Florida, to prepare for the invasion of Cuba, the local government made it clear that members of the all-black regiments were not to be distinguished from local black civilians, who lived under severe discrimination and segregation rules. Tensions there rose quickly, and so to minimize conflict with the locals, the Army forced the Buffalo Soldiers to board the transport vessel a week earlier than their white counterparts and to stay belowdecks in oppressive heat and humidity. During the voyage to Cuba, the Buffalo Soldiers had the least favorable quarters. Here is what one of them wrote at the time:

> After some miles of railroad travel and much hustling we were put on board the transport. I say *on board*, but it is simply because we cannot use the terms *under board*. We were huddled together below two other regiments and under the water line, in the dirtiest, closest, most sickening place imaginable. For about fifteen days we were on the water in this dirty hole, but being soldiers we were compelled to accept this without a murmur. We ate corn beef and canned tomatoes with our hard bread until we were anything but half way pleased. In the fifth or sixth day out to sea the water furnished us became muddy or dirty and well flavored with salt, and remained so during the rest of the journey. Then, the ship's cooks, knowing well our condition made it convenient to themselves to sell us a glass of clean ice water and a small piece of bread and tainted meat for the sum of seventy-five cents, or one dollar*, as the case might be.[5]
>
> * Note that a dollar in 1898 is equivalent to nearly $30 in 2019.

AFRICAN AMERICANS IN WORLD WAR II

Although the numbers of African American soldiers were sparse at the beginning of the war (fewer than 4,000 troops in 1941),[6] they increased steadily through enlistment and the draft. "By 1945, more than 1.2 million African Americans would be serving in uniform on the Home Front, in Europe, and the Pacific (including thousands of African American women in the Women's auxiliaries)."[7] More than 125,000 African Americans served overseas in World War II.[8]

With the exception of a few units that prepared for frontline combat from the beginning (the 92nd and 93rd Infantries, the 761st Tank Battalion, and the Tuskegee Airmen, among others), most African Americans were only allowed to serve in combat-support service units, usually as truck drivers and dockworkers. It was only during a critical manpower shortage at the Battle of the Bulge toward the end of the war that General Dwight D. Eisenhower allowed 2,000 African American soldiers the opportunity to form all-black units (but always under command of white officers) to help fill the short-falls in his depleted ranks. Additionally, they were forced back into combat-support roles as soon as adequate white replacements were available.

In many ways, discrimination against black servicemen and women had grown more severe by World War II than it had been during the Civil War. Still, trucks and ships needed to be loaded, food prepared, supplies moved forward, and vehicles and aircraft maintained; the fact that black Americans did these jobs well was an essential contribution to the Allied victory.

Sometimes, the best way to understand the contributions of many is to focus on the story of a few. Two black Americans who stand out for their service in World War II are the father-son pair of Benjamin O. Davis Senior and Benjamin O. Davis Junior. Davis Sr. became the first black American to achieve the rank of general in the United States Army. His son became the first black American to achieve the rank of general in the Air Force. As commander of the Tuskegee Airmen, nicknamed the Red Tails, Benjamin Davis Jr. made a unique and powerful impact on the European War.

BENJAMIN O. DAVIS JR. AND THE TUSKEGEE AIRMEN

A particular event of a racial nature that affected all of us is sharply etched in my memory. I call it the night of the Klan. About a mile and a half from

Tuskegee Institute, a new Veterans Administration Hospital for black veterans was soon to be completed. To express its preference that jobs for doctors and nurses go to whites instead of blacks, as was planned at the time, the Ku Klux Klan announced a full-scale march past the Institute. It is difficult today to appreciate fully the terror the Klan created in the minds of black people, but in the 1920s, particularly in Alabama and Mississippi, Klan lynchings still occurred frequently.

Our house and all the other houses in the immediate neighborhood were occupied by faculty and other employees of the Institute. Our official instructions were to stay indoors and turn off the lights to keep from provoking the marchers in any way. But as a Regular Army officer, my father refused to cower behind closed doors. Furthermore, he believed that the entire Davis family should make known its opinion of the Klan by staying visible and not hiding in the shadows. On the night of the Klan, therefore, Mother Sadie, my two sisters, and I sat quietly on our porch, my father resplendent in his white dress uniform, and the rest of us viewing the parade with some concern about what might happen when the Klansmen marched by. Our porch light was the only light to be seen for miles around except for the flaming torches of the Klansmen, who passed by on the street only a few feet from where we sat. Also resplendent in white—robes, masks, and hoods—they passed by without incident. In the end the Klan lost its fight, and the jobs went to blacks as originally planned. Today the hospital is staffed by both black and white doctors and nurses.[9]

At the time this event occurred in the early 1920s, Benjamin O. Davis Sr. was a professor of military science and tactics at the all-black Tuskegee Institute in Alabama. His willingness to risk his life, and the lives of his family, shows the courage he displayed in the face of segregation, which followed him all the days of his military career. In spite of the challenge of being a black officer in a mostly white army, he rose to the rank of brigadier general, the first African American to achieve that distinction. When his son was commissioned as a second lieutenant upon his graduation from the United States Military Academy at West Point in 1936, there were just two black commissioned officers in the United States Army: Benjamin Davis Sr. and Benjamin Davis Jr. Together, they helped break down the barriers that prevented African American men and women from achieving their full potential in military service.

But it was not easy. Benjamin Davis Jr. was only the fourth African American to graduate from West Point, and the first in the twentieth century. In the first few weeks there, a number of young cadets and even one upper classman reached out to him in kindness. But that changed one day after he inadvertently received a summons to a meeting in the basement of his dormitory:

> As I approached the assembly where the meeting was in progress, I heard someone ask, "What are we going to do about the nigger?" I realized then that the meeting was *about* me, and I was not supposed to attend. I turned on my heel and double-timed back to my room.
>
> From that meeting on, the cadets who roomed across the hall, who had been friendly earlier, no longer spoke to me. In fact, no one spoke to me except in the line of duty. Apparently, certain upperclass cadets had determined that I was getting along too well at the Academy to suit them, and they were going to enforce an old West Point tradition—"silencing"—with the object of making my life so unhappy that I would resign. Silencing had been applied in the past to certain

cadets who were considered to have violated the honor code and refused to resign. In my case there was no question of such a violation, which would have been formally cited by the Honor Committee; I was to be silenced solely because cadets did not want blacks at West Point. Their only purpose was to freeze me out. What they did not realize was that I was stubborn enough to put up with their treatment to reach the goal I had come to attain.[10]

The silent treatment was enforced on Davis for the entire four years he was in the academy. He lived without a roommate, was assigned to his own tent during field exercises, ate by himself at every meal, and was never spoken to by other cadets except for official communications. Only once did the cadets show him kindness, which was at the end of his first year (a point by which many men had resigned because of the rigor of the program), when many upperclassmen came up and shook his hand and told him he had done a good job. By the end of four years he graduated 35th in a class of 276—an outstanding accomplishment.[11]

Davis Jr. always wanted to become a pilot, but in spite of his terrific performance at the academy, he was turned down when he applied to the aviation program. The reason given was that there were not enough men to fill an all-black unit, and it was unthinkable that a black American could serve among whites. Like his father before him, Davis Jr. was assigned to a teaching position at Tuskegee so that he would not be placed in a position of commanding white troops. It looked very much like Davis Jr. would follow in his father's footsteps, in which he was given command position only over other black soldiers, never white, and not in combat. It was discouraging, but during the Great Depression he earned above-average income and housing, so he stayed with it.

Then things changed with the outbreak of war in Europe. Under political pressure to make better use of African American troops in the military, President Franklin D. Roosevelt ordered the creation of a black flying unit in 1941. The only active African American graduate of West Point, Davis Jr. was given command of this new unit. A new airfield and operations center was created in Tuskegee, Alabama, and white pilots came down to start training a small group of college-educated black volunteers to be pilots. Simultaneously, others with at least a high school education were trained in all support roles, including as mechanics, fuelers, dispatchers, and so on. This was heartening to Davis Jr. since it meant that his group, the 99th Pursuit Squadron, would benefit from the skills of highly educated and skilled team members. All who were assigned to training recognized early on that if they could learn to do well in combat, they could affect perceptions of black soldiers in all branches of the military; they worked tirelessly to learn the skills of flying, logistics, and combat.

The white citizens of Tuskegee were not happy to have a new airfield built so close to their town, as it changed the ratio of blacks to whites. They even petitioned their United States senators to have the unit broken up; but the War Department persisted until the camp was finished. Sadly, for the soldiers serving on the base, it was somewhat like living in a prison camp because they could not go into town for rest and relaxation.

When the group was finally called up to active duty, they departed for Tunisia in North Africa in the spring of 1943. In a first in service history, Lieutenant Colonel Davis was put in charge of all military personnel on the troopship, which included more than 3,000 white Army soldiers. While there wasn't much supervision required for the ten-day crossing, it was significant that a black American was finally given command of white troops, if even for a limited period of time.

The squadron went to work flying Curtiss P-40 fighters, seeing their first aerial combat on June 9, 1943, when they provided close air support to Allied bombers flying out over the Mediterranean.[12] Some shadowed the bombers, while others actively engaged the Germans in air-to-air combat. Tuskegee Airman Willie Ashley damaged one of the German aircraft, causing the German attack group to break off and head for home. It was their first victory in the air. They continued to engage the enemy, both in aerial combat and in dive-bombing missions against German ground positions on the island of Pantelleria. Once the Germans were subdued, the group prepared for the next advance in the war, which would take them to the island of Sicily. They were off to a good start:

> After the surrender of Pantelleria, Col. J. R. Hawkins, the area commander, wrote to me as follows: "I wish to extend to you and the members of the squadron my heartiest congratulations for the splendid part you played in the Pantelleria show. You have met the challenge of the enemy and have come out of your initial christening into battle stronger qualified than ever. Your people have borne up well under battle conditions and there is every reason to believe that with more experience you will take your place in the battle line along with the best of them."[13]

But controversy was brewing. In September 1943, Davis Jr. was recalled to the United States to assume command of 332nd Fighter Group, which consisted of three black squadrons with all supporting personnel. His job was to prepare this new group for combat. While in the United States, field commanders in Africa issued a report critical of the performance of black pilots in the eight months they had been in the Mediterranean, recommending that they lacked the proper fighting spirit as well as the quick reflexes required for air combat. The recommendation was that they be relegated to non-combat reconnaissance and support flying. Naturally, this infuriated

Benjamin Davis Jr., who held a press conference at the Pentagon to refute the allegations. *Time* magazine reported on the controversy with the conclusion that the 99th was "only a single facet of the Army's problem to train and use black troops," and "most thoughtful Army officers probably would agree that blacks would never develop potentialities as an airman or other soldier under the system of segregation in training."[14]

The fate of the black airmen desperate to establish their credibility in combat roles as equal to whites hung in the balance. Fortunately, General Hap Arnold of the Army and General George C. Marshall, chairman of the Joint Chiefs of Staff, put the recommendation on hold, allowing the 99th to continue combat operations. Soon, the official report of the inquiry concluded that "an examination of the record of the 99th Fighter Squadron reveals no significant general difference between this squadron and the balance of the P-40 squadrons in the Mediterranean Theater Operations."[15] In spite of the prejudice that attempted to silence them, the 99th was vindicated. Davis Jr. wrote:

> All those who wished to denigrate the quality of the 99th's operations were silenced once and for all by its aerial victories over Anzio on two successive days in January 1944. Eight enemy fighters were downed on 27 January, and four more were destroyed the next day. There would be no more talk of lack of aggressiveness, absence of teamwork, or disintegrating under fire. The 99th was finally achieving recognition as a superb tactical fighter unit, an expert in putting bombs on designated targets, and a unit of acknowledged superiority in aerial combat with the Luftwaffe.[16]

The Tuskegee Airmen, who earned the nickname "The Red Tails" for the distinctive markings on the tails of their aircraft, became celebrated heroes of aerial combat, particularly by the American bomber crews who noted that the black fighter pilots stayed with them through the most hazardous parts of the bombing run, while most other pilots broke off when ground-based flak became most intense. During World War II, the airmen commanded by Davis Jr. flew more than 15,000 sorties, shot down 111 enemy planes, and destroyed 273 on the ground. They lost 66 aircraft. More than 14,000 African Americans served in the Army Air Corps, of which 1,000 were pilots, the rest serving as navigators, bombardiers, radio operators, weathermen, and ground-based crews.[17]

Benjamin Davis Jr. went on to serve a distinguished military career. He transferred from the Army to the Air Force when it became an independent military service in 1947. He saw additional combat flying the F-86 Sabre in the Korean War. In the following decades he assumed various domestic and overseas commands, achieving the temporary rank of general while in Tokyo in 1954. In 1957 he was made chief of staff of the Twelfth Air Force at Ramstein Air Base, Germany. His appointment to brigadier general was made permanent in 1960, making him the first African American in Air Force history to achieve that rank. He retired from active-duty service in 1970 and was promoted to a four-star insignia, retired, in 1998 by President Bill Clinton. His was a distinguished and exemplary career that paved the way for thousands of other African Americans to serve in leadership positions in the military. In some ways, the path he and his father forged is incredible—the only two commissioned African American officers in the United States in 1936 who ultimately commanded tens of thousands of servicemen worldwide.

DESEGREGATION OF THE ARMED FORCES BY EXECUTIVE ORDER IN 1948

Benjamin Davis Sr. retired from the military in a public ceremony on July 20, 1948, after serving fifty years in the United States Army. This ceremony was presided over by President Harry S.

Truman. Six days later, on July 26, 1948, President Truman issued Executive Order 9981, which abolished racial discrimination and segregation in the United States Armed Forces.

Today, seventy years later, all men and women serve side by side regardless of race. Once one of the most strictly segregated institutions in society, the United States military is now among the most accepting. While racial prejudice undoubtedly still exists, it is not institutional in nature.

What is clear from history is that the valor and loyalty of African Americans in the military should never have been called into question in the first place. In the battles of the Revolutionary War, the Civil War, the Plains Wars, the Spanish American-War, and the World Wars, they fought bravely and ferociously—in all respects the equal of others. Through their courageous acts, often while suffering from severe racial discrimination, they brought distinction to the United States uniformed services in which they served and to the country in which they and their families lived.

CHAPTER 10

ROSIE THE RIVETER

WOMEN IN THE WAR INDUSTRIES

Nineteen million American women were employed at the height of production in World War II, more than three million in war-related industries.[1] More than 310,000 women worked in the aircraft industry in 1943, making up 65 percent of the total employed in that field. Before the war, women had made up just 1 percent of that specialized workforce.[2] And it wasn't just in the United States that women stepped forward to take on roles traditionally reserved for men. In Great Britain, where the war was literally a life-and-death struggle for the survival of their nation, a remarkable seven out of eight women had wartime jobs.[3]

As the demand for both skilled and unskilled workers soared with full mobilization, women stepped forward to meet the need. In doing so, they shattered the myth that women couldn't do "a man's job" in heavy industry and other skilled occupations. While this was a source of pride during the war, it became a point of contention after the war when men returned home from the battlefields, anxious to take up their old jobs, many of which had been assumed by women. While many women were happy to step aside and return home, particularly married women with children, not all were pleased to be displaced back into lower-paid, lower-skilled work that failed to utilize the full range of their talents. Regardless, the overall percentage of women in the workforce fell quickly at the end of hostilities in 1945, and average women's pay slumped as women returned to more traditional roles such as teaching and nursing. Female workers were crucial to victory, and the effect their service had on women's roles in the workforce is still being felt today.

It should also be noted that more than 350,000 women served directly in support of the military, including the Women's Army Corps (WACs), Women's Airforce Service Pilots (WASPs), Women Accepted for Voluntary Military Services (WAVES), and the SPARs[4] who supported the Coast Guard.[5]

THE BIRTH OF ROSIE THE RIVETER

Like Athena springing full-grown from the forehead of Zeus, Rosie the Riveter was born full-grown in 1942 when the musical group the Four Vagabonds released a new recording, "Rosie the Riveter." It was an instant sensation, fueling the public's imagination with the idea of a tough but practical young woman who stepped forward to fight for victory. Not only did Rosie do a man's job in the aircraft factory, she loved her boyfriend, Charlie, a Marine, and worked to keep him safe. With her extra earnings, Rosie bought war bonds to finance the war; and the result of her hard work was that Moscow (an American ally) cheered her accomplishments while the Nazis in Berlin trembled in fear. The first stanza says it best:

> *All the day long, whether rain or shine*
> *She's a part of the assembly line*
> *She's making history, working for victory*
> *Rosie, brrrrrrrrrr, the riveter.*[6]

The release of this song was the debut of the name "Rosie the Riveter." The real-life inspiration for the lyrics is said to be the wealthy Rosalind P. Walter, who worked a night shift building the F4U Corsair fighter. Another woman, Rose Will Monroe, also became associated with the moniker. She worked as a riveter building B-24 bombers in the Willow Run aircraft factory in Michigan.

People quickly understood that Rosie represented all the women who gave up home and hearth to go to work in the factories doing hard physical labor building tanks, aircraft, ships, bombs, and ammunition to supply the men in the field. They welded and riveted, drilled and folded, filled bullets and lined aviation fuel tanks with rubber, and performed every other task required to fuel America's war machine, including in the female auxiliaries of the Army and Navy, the WACs and the WAVEs.

Of course, not all women worked directly in war industries. Many stepped into clerical and other jobs vacated by men in all areas of the economy, helping to keep the country running. Some went to work on farms driving tractors and bringing in the crops. Others worked in shipping to get needed goods to both civilian and military destinations. As the war intensified, more and more women were actively recruited to leave their homes to fill needed positions. When the pool of available unmarried women was fully employed, recruiting turned to married women. This required daycare for their children, which was sometimes provided by older relatives but often happened in onsite kindergartens and daycare centers. Thus did Rosie transform the role of working mothers and their place in society.

One of the most positive aspects of Rosie and her sisters is that they broke down racial and economic barriers. White women soon worked alongside Latina and African American women, forming friendships that would have been unlikely before the war.

ROSIE BECOMES REAL

Today, most people associate Rosie with two iconic posters from World War II. The first shows a beautiful but tough young woman with a red bandanna against a bright yellow background flexing her arm under the words, "We Can Do It!" This poster is often associated with Rosie. Originally, however, it was a motivational poster designed by artist J. Howard Miller, hired by a committee at the Westinghouse Company to create promotional artwork for the war effort. It ended up being used for only two weeks, and then only internally, at Westinghouse offices in the Midwest. In the 1980s it was rediscovered and used as a symbol of the women's movement and was only then associated with "Rosie the Riveter." The poster's image was likely derived from a photo of a lathe operator, Naomi Parker, taken at the Alameda Naval Air Station in California in 1942.[7]

The second poster, which gained its fame during the war, was painted by Norman Rockwell and appeared on the cover of the *Saturday Evening Post* on Memorial Day, May 29, 1943. Rockwell's image was based on photos of a Vermont girl, nineteen-year-old Mary Doyle, a telephone operator who lived near the famous illustrator.[8] Rockwell's image shows a saucy young woman with red hair and bulging muscles, a pair of goggles tucked back on her brow, and a rivet gun laying across her legs. Rockwell's Rosie wore blue coveralls and had her feet planted firmly on a copy of Adolf Hitler's *Mein Kampf* to indicate that she was going to pound him into the ground. So popular was Rockwell's Rosie that sales of that issue of the *Post* were nearly double its usual sales. The *Post* soon loaned the image to the US Treasury Department, who distributed thousands of posters around the country to sell war bonds.[9]

Hollywood also recognized the power of this new icon and moved quickly to film a new movie, *Rosie the Riveter*, starring Jane

Frazee as Rosie Warren, a young woman who shared a room in a crowded boarding house with her best friend, Vera Watson (played by Barbara Allen), as they worked in a defense plant in Southern California.[10]

ROSIE IN REAL LIFE

Today we know the outcome of the war—American industrial might churned out war matériel in quantities unknown and unimagined before. Our factories supplied not only US troops but English and Russian troops as well. As an example, American aircraft production went from less than 3,000 in 1939 to 300,000 by 1945, each built with 65 percent female labor.

But all of that was unknown in 1942 when Rosie came on the scene. The Pacific fleet had been destroyed in Pearl Harbor, and the Philippine Islands had fallen to the Japanese early in the year. Germany was triumphant in Europe. British home islands faced the threat of starvation because of German U-boat attacks on supply convoys. In other words, there was real anxiety about the Allies' ability to respond to Germany and Japan in time to make a difference. Every woman who went to work freed up a man to join the military. The need was so urgent in England that they imposed a draft on women to fill the factories. In North America, the promise of a higher wage and new skills caused many women to move out of low-paying jobs into the higher-wage jobs of war production. Others stepped forward out of patriotism. For many, their service in the war industries was life changing, and they came to see themselves in a new and positive light. Of course, there are millions of stories of women whose lives were affected by employment during the war. Here are three that are representative of what it was like to be a woman in the defense industry.

RACHEL HINSZ SAGMILLER

Rachel Sagmiller was restless in the home she shared with five siblings on the plains in her hometown of Zap, North Dakota. Right after graduating from high school, she left Zap to go to work in a defense factory. This story is derived from a small memoir her son, G. Sagmiller, wrote about his conversations with his mother after the war.[11]

When war broke out in the Pacific, a friend encouraged Rachel to head west to Seattle with her. It was her friend's idea to join the other 350,000 women who eventually enlisted in a female military auxiliary, like the Women's Army Corps (WAC) or the Women Accepted for Voluntary Emergency Service (WAVES) in the Navy, but Rachel did not like the idea of people telling her what to do. So instead, they headed west to Seattle, leaving North Dakota for the first time in their lives to go to work for Boeing. To her dismay, Boeing wasn't hiring, so Rachel went to work filling packing crates for the Navy. They helped load the supplies a naval ship would need while cruising, and she loved seeing the names of the ships stamped on the outside of the wooden crates, particularly since the battleships were named for the states in the Union. This job lasted through the summer, and then she returned home when her friend was offered a teaching job back in North Dakota.

By the next summer she wanted to get back to the big city and to earn the high pay available in manufacturing. So she talked her sister and another young woman into joining her. This time she was able to find a job as a riveter in the huge Boeing factory, where she worked on B-17 and B-29 bombers. One of the things that struck her as interesting was that the whole huge factory complex was covered by massive camouflage nets to conceal it from a potential Japanese air attack. Another was that only one-half of the bomber was built at her factory; the second half was built at a factory in the midwestern United States, and the two halves were put together at a third factory. The strategy behind this arrangement was that if one factory was bombed, they'd lose only half an airplane rather than the whole thing.

Rachel's first job was as a riveter, the same as the fictional Rosie. Here's how she described the work to her son:

> Mom also told me that while she worked in multiple parts of the plant, she started out as a rivet holder. She'd get a hot bucket of rivets, go inside the plane, and hold them in place while someone on the outside of the plane hit them. Every night when she went home, her ears would ring for hours. It was very loud being in that plane when someone was pounding rivets from the outside. I think she did lose a lot of her hearing while doing this job. She'd always have trouble hearing us when we talked, especially when she wasn't able to see our mouths. Later in life, she needed hearing aids.[12]

A rivet is a permanent fastener made from steel to hold two pieces of metal together. The rivet has a smooth shaft with a rounded head on one end. After the rivet is heated until it is glowing hot, it is driven into predrilled holes and then the tail end of the shaft is quickly pounded by a hammer or air gun until it deforms into a second head at the opposite end. The heating and cooling of the rivet causes it to wedge tightly in the holes to create a permanent bond. Because the rivet is a single piece of steel, it has high structural strength and dependability. But handling the glowing, heated rivets and pounding the tail until it forms a second head is both noisy and hot.

In the evenings, Rachel loved to dance, and she spent part of her hard-earned income to buy stylish clothes and dance heels. She also formed lifelong friendships with the other women who worked alongside her. Eventually she advanced from rivet-holder to rivet-runner, which required her to carry buckets of red-hot rivets from the furnace to the assembly-line workers. If the rivets cooled while waiting to be placed, she had to lug them back to the furnace to be reheated. This work required both muscles and stamina. Rachel was popular with the other women and enjoyed the work for as long as she could tolerate the noise. Eventually she started getting severe headaches, which convinced her it was time to go home to North Dakota. The war ended, and she built a life of her own, but she always recalled with fondness her time as a real-life Rosie the Riveter.

VERONICA FOSTER— RONNIE THE BREN GUN GIRL

Canada declared war on Germany on September 10, 1939, fully two years before the United States entered the war, so the need to ramp up their war industries came earlier than it did in the United States. The National Film Board of Canada decided to create a recruiting campaign to attract women into industry. Rather than use a professional actress or model, they started a search to find an attractive, self-confident woman already working in the war industry. They found her assembling Bren light machine guns at the Inglis manufacturing plant in Toronto. A Bren gun was a rapid-fire machine gun used by British and Commonwealth troops. The woman they found was the dark-haired Veronica Foster, who was just seventeen years old at the outbreak of war. She was the perfect real-life woman to inspire the country, given that her three brothers had all enlisted in the Canadian military and gone off to war. Here was a family that was giving their all for the common good.

No one had ever called Veronica "Ronnie" in real life, but the Film Board thought it had broader appeal to fashion their recruiting icon as "Ronnie, the Bren Gun Girl." The Canadian campaign was far broader in focus than the US Rosie promotions that came two years later. Rosie was exclusively depicted at work in an airplane factory; but a film crew followed Veronica for several days to capture multiple elements of her life. During the day she was shown as the hardworking, strong assembly-line worker hefting twenty-four-pound, forty-eight-inch long Bren guns at the final point of assembly. But unlike Rosie, who was always depicted already at work, the promotional photos and film reels showed Ronnie getting ready to work by tying up her hair and covering it with her trademark bandanna (men wore hats, women bandannas), putting on lipstick, and doing her best to look both attractive and strong. Then they followed her home, where she put on stylish clothes to go out dancing and to dinner. The goal was to show that a woman could be both an excellent worker and an attractive companion for the young men in her life, and that with the higher wages paid in defense, she could afford it.

The recruiting drive was a smashing success, and Ronnie was soon recognized all over Canada. More than 800,000 women accepted the call to work in munitions and equipment factories. Veronica and the 14,000 other Bren Gun Girls who worked at the Inglis plant produced more than 40,000 weapons over the course of the war. Their contribution was considered invaluable.[13]

However, just as soon as the war in Europe ended in 1945, all of the women were laid off so the plant could be converted back to its original purpose of making pumps and other machinery. Women all over Canada found out that their employers had considered them temporary workers, with no intention of offering them permanent positions after the war. This caused financial hardship for many.

As for Ronnie, she largely disappeared from the nation's consciousness. But Veronica Foster did not. She capitalized on her good looks and experience as "Ronnie" to work as a model and then later as lead singer in the Canadian big band "Mart Kenney and His Western Gentlemen." This band was popular all over Canada, and

Veronica's voice was heard over the radio and in recordings. It was while she was in the band that she met her future husband, George Guerette, a professional trombone player. Together they raised five children.

Some liberties were taken in creating the character of Ronnie. For example, Veronica, as Ronnie, was shown smoking a cigarette while sitting on an assembly table examining a recently completed Bren gun. Her daughter said later that her mother never used tobacco in real life, but at the time smoking was considered both suave and manly—characteristics that the Film Board considered attractive in their tough-as-nails but soft and feminine Ronnie.[14]

As of this writing, there is an excellent YouTube video that tells the story of Veronica and Ronnie and includes clips of her singing on the radio. It shows photos from throughout her life, from her days as a beautiful young model to her years as a loving mother and finally a gracious elderly woman.[15] Veronica Foster Guerette passed away in 2000 at the age of seventy-eight.

CHARLCIA NEUMEN

Charlcia Neumen was married and living near a Lockheed factory in California when the war broke out. Her husband had a relatively low-paying job with the local school board, so she was open to a neighbor's suggestion that they look into employment at the aircraft plant. Her husband was against it. Her younger brother and her father were even more adamant that she shouldn't "work amongst people like that."[16] Charlcia realized that the other workers were people just like her, so she paid no heed to the men who resisted.

The first step was to go to the nearby Vultee factory to be tested for dexterity and adaptability. Charlcia tested near the very top of the class, later saying, "See, anything using my hands—I could take a little hand drill and go up and down these holes as fast as you could move, just go like that, where most people would break a drill. It was a very simple thing. The riveting is the same way. It's just a matter of rhythm. So it was easy to do."[17]

Charlcia's eye for precision and her steady hand qualified her to mark and drill holes on the ribs of a Lockheed P-38 fuselage assembly. The P-38 was a versatile twin-engine aircraft used for multiple applications, including enemy interception, dive bombing, level bombing, air reconnaissance and photography, and night fighting. Such missions required an aircraft with great strength since incredible stress would be placed on the structural components of the aircraft, particularly on dive bombing operations. Thus, it was critical that the rivets were perfectly placed and seated:

> The P-38 that Lockheed put out was a twin en-gine, and we worked on the center part between the two hulls. It was a much heavier rivet that went into this. It was what they called cold riveting; you took them out of the icebox real cold and riveted it. That was harder work. Well, the jig would be empty, see, so the first job would be to mark your ribs. We took a red pencil and just put a line right down through the center. That was so that when we pushed it into position, then, we could be sure we were hitting the center of the rib when we drilled. You'd ruin the whole rib if you've got too much in the curve or something like that. So we fastened the ribs in; then we put the skin on and fastened the Cleco clamps on it. The jig was in place so we could drill it. We marked along the edges so we could trim it, and then we took it off and trimmed the excess piece. We put it back together again and riveted up, and then we'd loosen the whole thing and take it off and put it in a special holder to be inspected for bad rivets. After inspection, it went to the next two girls and they added the next part."[18]

That was Charlcia's job, and she did it throughout the war. The extra income allowed her and her husband to pay off the mortgage on their home. Plus, she took pride in the role she played in making the safest aircraft possible for the men who went into combat.

While employed she worked six or seven days a week from 7:00 A.M. until 4:00 P.M., and then had to go home and make supper for her family. Her husband was good to help with housework, but much of the burden for caring for her family still rested on her shoulders.

When the war ended, Charlcia accepted her layoff with grace. She knew going into the job that it was temporary, and she was one of the women who felt it was all right to allow the returning servicemen to take up the jobs. She was tired and ready to go home. But she also acknowledged that not all her coworkers felt that way. They liked the work and would have stayed at it if given the chance. She felt that in some ways she had crossed an important line that opened up more opportunities and choices for her daughter and other young women when they reached adulthood. In the end, Charlcia viewed her work as a very positive episode in her life:

> It was a very good experience for me because of the challenge of doing something like that, to prove to myself that I could do it. And working with all the different types of people—I'd always been very shy about meeting people. Actually, I was afraid of going out and asking for a job because I didn't think I could do it. So I found out I could do it; it was the type of thing that I could do, that I liked to do. I had a natural knack. There again, the rhythm of riveting is natural. You know if you're good at tools and good in using your hands, your eye and hand coordination is good then. And riveting is a very easy thing for a woman to do.[19]

IMPACT OF ROSIE THE RIVETER

Though postwar employment for women receded, Rosie and her sisters left a lasting impact on America. In January of 1942, employers estimated that just 29 percent of available jobs were suitable for women. Six months later that proportion was raised to 85 percent. As women moved into these jobs they soon proved that not only were the jobs suitable for them, but the women were also, in every respect, equal to the challenges of the jobs. This simple change in attitude on the part of employers and women opened thousands of new job opportunities for women in the decades following the war.

Wartime employment of women also had a salutary, if disproportionate, effect on the lives of women from minority populations. Prior to the war they were almost universally consigned to menial jobs with little or no opportunity for advancement. But the demands of war opened up opportunities for women of all ethnic backgrounds to work side-by-side on the assembly lines, in offices, and in hospital wards with each other. This also contributed to greater equality in employment and social status following the war. Finally, in the 1980s, Rosie became a symbol of women asserting their rights to equal opportunity and equal pay in employment—a goal that is not yet fully reached but is far more attainable than it was in 1941.

FINAL THOUGHTS

It has been a moving experience to research and write about the individuals and groups who are featured in this book. I personally interviewed Pat Patton and admire his courage and humanity. It took many years for Pat to forgive his Japanese captors and let go of his bitterness, but eventually he succeeded.

I also have an indirect connection to Hyalmar Anderson in that his nephew, Lloyd Kartchner, is one of my best friends. After writing the chapter on Hyalmar's accident and disappearance, Lloyd read it and then told me that even fifty years after the fact his mother still wept when she thought about her long-lost brother. She shared that grief with the tens of thousands of other families whose sons were classified as missing in action.

By far the most surprising story I researched was that of Dickey Chapelle. My goodness, was she an entertaining and lively author. I rank her book as one of the most interesting books I've ever read, and I've read thousands of books. Her memoir captured so much that is admirable in the men and women who serve in the military; the loyalty they have for each other, the resilience they display even when in terrible pain, and the respect with which they treated a woman who was brave enough to join them in battle. Her book, *What's a Woman Doing Here? A Reporter's Report on Herself*, went out of print many years ago but has been resurrected by a group called Scholar Select who scanned a used copy of the book from the Kansas City Public Library. I was fortunate to get a copy of this reproduction and now consider it a great treasure in my library. I always knew that combat photographers and journalists were brave, but Dickey Chapelle took my understanding to a whole new level.

I was deeply moved by the pathos of young, second-generation Japanese Americans fighting bravely in Europe while their families were imprisoned back in America for no justifiable reason. I enjoyed studying about the groups of people who served without full recognition, including combat engineers; African American soldiers, many or most of whom were not allowed a combat role; as well as the women who served in various capacities, from factory workers to resistance commanders.

Two other chapters affected me in a surprising way: the one on Joseph Medicine Crow and the one about Navajo code talkers. I grew up near the Blackfoot Indian Reservation in southeastern Idaho (as it was called then) and went to school with many First Americans. Even by second grade I marveled at their artistic skills and unique camaraderie. But as a child I felt the wariness we felt for each other. In researching the two stories included here I gained a far deeper respect for Native American traditions and culture. Chester Nez was happy in his childhood home, even though it lacked electricity and running water. He and his family had deep respect for nature and for each other and were taught to see beauty in everything about them. Chief Medicine Crow also held values that are inspiring. I'm glad I came to know these remarkable people better and to learn important life lessons from their cultures.

And so it goes. In so many ways I love each of the stories in this book, as well as its companion book, *Compassionate Soldier: Remarkable True Stories of Mercy, Heroism, and Honor from the Battlefield.* Both were researched and written at the request of Chris Schoebinger, Heidi Taylor, and their associates at Shadow Mountain. I consider it a great honor to give new life to the stories of the remarkable people featured here.

For more information on my books of military history, both fiction and nonfiction, I encourage you to visit www.jerryborrowman .com. If you do, I'd love to hear from you.

NOTES

CHAPTER 1: PAT PATTON

1. Henry Robert Patton, interview with author.
2. The letter in front of the number describes the purpose of the aircraft. For example, *O* stands for Observation, *B* for Bomber, and *F* for Fighter.
3. MacArthur and his staff traveled by boat to Mindanao, then by airplane to Australia.
4. There is no official record of how many men died during the Bataan Death March. An unknown number of men—both American and Filipino—refused to surrender and escaped to the jungle instead. Estimates for the number of men who were forced on the march vary widely, as do eyewitness accounts of the march. Differing sources estimate 5,000 to as many as 18,000 Filipino deaths and 500 to 650 American deaths. (See Michael and Elizabeth Norman, *Tears in the Darkness*.)

CHAPTER 2: NANCY WAKE

1. Mick Joffe Caricatures, "Nancy Wake, the White Mouse," August 13, 2011.
2. Mick Joffe Caricatures, "Nancy Wake, the White Mouse."
3. Kathryn J. Atwood, *Women Heroes of World War II*, 181.
4. Atwood, *Women Heroes of World War II*, 181–82.
5. Paul Vitello, "Nancy Wake, Proud Spy and Nazi Foe, Dies at 98."
6. Russell Braddon, *Nancy Wake*, loc. 86 of 4196.
7. Braddon, *Nancy Wake*, loc. 1383–92 of 4196.
8. Braddon, *Nancy Wake*, loc. 2532 and 2915 of 4196.
9. Braddon, *Nancy Wake*, loc. 4092–4104 of 4196.

CHAPTER 3: JOSEPH HYALMAR ANDERSON

1. See *Defense POW/MIA Accounting Agency*, "Past Conflicts."
2. Dining halls at every US military base have on display a small, round table topped with a white tablecloth and decorated with symbols to memorialize missing brothers and sisters in arms. The white tablecloth represents the purity of the missing's response to the country's call to arms. The empty chair represents the unknown faces not present. The round table represents neverending concern for the missing. A Bible represents faith in a higher power. A black napkin represents the emptiness left in the hearts of loved ones. A single red rose represents the families of those missing. A yellow candle represents everlasting hope for a joyous reunion. Lemon slices on the bread plate represent the bitter fate of those MIA. The salt on the bread plate represents the tears of the missing's families. An upside-down wine glass represents the sad truth that lost comrades are not there to share a drink or a toast. (See *Navy Life*, "The POW/MIA Table: A Place Setting for One, a Table for All.")
3. Bertha Kartchner, *Memories of Hyalmar Anderson*. Bertha is Hyalmar's younger sister by two years.
4. Joseph Hyalmar Anderson, "My Service Diary," 1.
5. Letter from James Forrestal to Joseph A. Anderson.
6. Joseph H. Anderson to Ruth Botel, March 6, 2000.
7. Ruth Botel, "Plane Lost at Lawn Point during WWII"; "Fishermen Watch Scope Sink at Sea."
8. *Contrails*, "Ventura Crew Remembered," July 2005; see also *Contrails*, "The Story of the US Navy Ventura PV-1 28736," July 2005.
9. Lloyd Kartchner to Jerry Borrowman, email correspondence, July 17, 2017.
10. Emily Dickinson, *Poems of Emily Dickinson*, 59.

CHAPTER 4: JOSEPH MEDICINE CROW

1. Joseph Medicine Crow, *Counting Coup*, 10–12.
2. Medicine Crow, *Counting Coup*, 102.
3. Throughout his two published books, Joseph Medicine Crow identifies his people as Indians, and indicates that he lived on an Indian reservation. I will use that term while quoting him in this story, but the term "Native American(s)" elsewhere.

4. Joseph Medicine Crow, *From the Heart of the Crow Country*, 12.

5. Joseph Medicine Crow, *Counting Coup*, 28–29.

6. Medicine Crow, *From the Heart of the Crow Country*, 44.

7. Medicine Crow, *Counting Coup*, 81.

8. Medicine Crow, *Counting Coup*, 84.

9. Medicine Crow, *Counting Coup*, 74.

10. Medicine Crow, *Counting Coup*, 98.

11. Medicine Crow, *Counting Coup*, 104–17.

12. Medicine Crow, *Counting Coup*, 123.

13. Medicine Crow, *Counting Coup*, 123.

14. Alison R. Bernstein, *American Indians and World War II*, 40.

15. Mike McPhate, "Joseph Medicine Crow, Tribal War Chief and Historian Dies at 102."

CHAPTER 5: DICKEY CHAPELLE

1. Penny Colman, *Where the Action Was,* viii.

2. Dickey Chapelle, *What's a Woman Doing Here?* 16.

3. Chapelle, *What's a Woman Doing Here?* 18.

4. Chapelle, *What's a Woman Doing Here?* 32.

5. Chapelle, *What's a Woman Doing Here?* 43–44.

6. Chapelle, *What's a Woman Doing Here?* 45.

7. Chapelle, *What's a Woman Doing Here?* 46–48.

8. Chapelle, *What's a Woman Doing Here?* 49.

9. Chapelle, *What's a Woman Doing Here?* 49.

10. Chapelle, *What's a Woman Doing Here?* 51.

11. Chapelle, *What's a Woman Doing Here?* 49–50.

12. Chapelle, *What's a Woman Doing Here?* 51–52.

13. Chapelle, *What's a Woman Doing Here?* 63.

14. Chapelle, *What's a Woman Doing Here?* 64.

15. See Chapelle, *What's a Woman Doing Here?* 64.

16. Chapelle, *What's a Woman Doing Here?* 65.

17. Chapelle, *What's a Woman Doing Here?* 67.

18. Chapelle, *What's a Woman Doing Here?* 76–77.

19. Chapelle, *What's a Woman Doing Here?* 78–79.

20. Chapelle, *What's a Woman Doing Here?* 81–82.

21. Chapelle, *What's a Woman Doing Here?* 118–19.

22. Chapelle, *What's a Woman Doing Here?* 120.

23. Chapelle, *What's a Woman Doing Here?* 123–24.
24. Chapelle, *What's a Woman Doing Here?* 140–41.
25. Chapelle, *What's a Woman Doing Here?* 181, 182.
26. Chapelle, *What's a Woman Doing Here?* 217.
27. Jackie Spinner, "Remembering 'Fearless' War Photographer."
28. Spinner, "Remembering 'Fearless' War Photographer."
29. "The Bill of Rights: A Transcription."

CHAPTER 6: NAVAJO CODE TALKERS

1. Chester Nez, *Code Talker*, 10, 12.
2. James Minahan, *Ethnic Groups of the Americas*, 262.
3. Nez, *Code Talker*, 131–32.
4. *Naval History and Heritage Command*, "Navajo Code Talkers: World War II Fact Sheet."
5. See *CNN.com*, "Navajo code talkers honored after 56 years."
6. Nez, *Code Talker*, 36.
7. See Nez, *Code Talker*, 78–80.
8. Nez, *Code Talker*, 50–51.
9. Nez, *Code Talker*, 84–85.
10. Nez, *Code Talker*, 97.
11. Nathan Aaseng, *Navajo Code Talkers*, 55–56.
12. Aaseng, *Navajo Code Talkers*, 100–101.
13. Nez, *Code Talker*, 217–18.
14. White House, "Remarks by the President in a Ceremony Honoring the Navajo Code Talkers."

CHAPTER 7: THE PURPLE HEART BATTALION

1. 1st Battalion, 141st Regiment, 36th Texas Infantry Division, United States Fifth Army.
2. See, for example, *Densho Encyclopedia*, "Rescue of the Lost Battalion."
3. Of the twenty-one Medals of Honor awarded to Japanese American soldiers serving in the 100th/442d, only one was awarded immediately after the war. The remaining twenty were awarded by President Bill Clinton on 21 June 2000 (see Robert Asahina, *Just Americans*, 7–8).
4. Joni L. Parker, "Nisei Soliders in WWII: The Campaign in the Vosges Mountains," 21–22.

5. Those of Japanese descent in Hawaii were not treated similarly, despite more than 40 percent of the Hawaiian population being of Japanese descent. Instead, Japanese Americans there were investigated, resulting in about 1,000 being detained.

6. See *Personal Justice Denied: Report of the Commission on Wartime Relocation and Internment of Civilians.*

7. General John L. DeWitt, testimony given April 13, 1943, before the House Naval Affairs Subcommittee, as cited in *Korematsu v. United States*, 323 US 214 (1944).

8. The 100th Infantry Battalion became one of three battalions in the 442d RCT; Parker, "Nisei Soldiers in WWII," 23.

9. C. Douglas Sterner, *Go for Broke*, 83–84.

10. Asahina, *Just Americans*, 191–92.

11. See Lyn Crost, *Honor by Fire*, 197.

12. Asahina, *Just Americans*, 202.

13. See, for example, Asahina, *Just Americans*, 198.

14. George H. W. Bush, "Remarks to World War II Veterans and Families in Honolulu, Hawaii," 7 December 1991.

CHAPTER 8: COMBAT ENGINEERS

1. Von Holger Willcke, "The 'Beer Bridge' Is Still Famous Today."

2. See David E. Pergrin and Eric M. Hammel, *First across the Rhine*, 295–97.

3. *Think Defence*, "UK Military Bridging—Equipment (The Bailey Bridge)."

4. The actual length of the Rhine is difficult to measure objectively. For decades, its length was listed as 820 miles. In 2010, however, it was listed closer to 765 miles by the Dutch Rijkswaterstaat, part of the Dutch Ministry of Infrastructure and Water Management. The Upper Rhine, which includes a portion of the Franco-German border, is 225 miles in length. In total, the Rhine passes through (or forms the border of) nearly 500 miles of German territory.

5. Pergrin and Hammel, *First across the Rhine*, 240.

6. Pergrin and Hammel, *First across the Rhine*, 241.

7. Pergrin and Hammel, *First across the Rhine*, 241.

8. Pergrin and Hammel, *First across the Rhine*, 256–57.

9. Pergrin and Hammel, *First across the Rhine*, 273.

10. Pergrin and Hammel, *First across the Rhine*, 274.
11. Pergrin and Hammel, *First across the Rhine*, 285–86.
12. Jay Divine, *Combat Engineer, Pacific Theater*.

CHAPTER 9: AFRICAN AMERICANS AT WAR

1. See *American Battlefield Trust*, "American Revolution—FAQs."
2. *Educator Resources of the National Archives*, "Black Soldiers in the US Military during the Civil War."
3. *GlobalSecurity.org*, "7th Squadron, 10th Cavalry Regiment."
4. *Harry S. Truman Presidential Library and Museum*, "Desegregation of the Armed Forces."
5. T. G. Steward, *Buffalo Soldiers*, 116–17.
6. *National World War II Museum*, "African Americans in World War II: Fighting for a Double Victory."
7. *National World War II Museum*, "African Americans in World War II."
8. See Ulysses Lee, *The Employment of Negro Troops*, chapter 21.
9. Benjamin O. Davis Jr., *Benjamin O. Davis, Jr.: American*, 11–12.
10. Davis, *Benjamin O. Davis, Jr.*, 27.
11. Davis, *Benjamin O. Davis, Jr.*, 48.
12. Davis, *Benjamin O. Davis, Jr.*, 101.
13. Davis, *Benjamin O. Davis, Jr.*, 101.
14. Davis, *Benjamin O. Davis, Jr.*, 106.
15. Davis, *Benjamin O. Davis, Jr.*, 107.
16. Davis, *Benjamin O. Davis, Jr.*, 107–8.
17. *Airforce Magazine*, "Red Tails, the Tuskegee Airman in Photos."

CHAPTER 10: ROSIE THE RIVETER

1. See Susan M. Hartmann, *The Homefront and Beyond*, 21.
2. *History.com*, "American Women in World War II."
3. Jane Waller and Michael Vaughan-Rees, *Women in Wartime*, 58.
4. SPARs stands for "*Semper Paratus*—Always Ready," the motto of the US Coast Guard.
5. See *Minnesota History Center*, "Women in the Military: World War II—Overview."
6. See Redd Evans and John Jacob Loeb, "Rosie the Riveter," for full lyrics.
7. See Tiare Dunlap, "Rosie the Riveter at 95." As the "We Can Do It!" poster found a new audience during the women's rights movements,

the model for the poster was originally misidentified. As noted in the story, Naomi Parker was the self-confident woman used for the image. Today she is best known by her last married name, Naomi Parker Fraley. She passed away on January 20, 2018.

8. David Hackett Fischer, *Liberty and Freedom*, 537–38.

9. Doris Weatherford, *American Women during World War II*, 399.

10. The movie was released in April 1944 and titled *Rosie the Riveter.*

11. See Girard Sagmiller, *We Can Do It!*

12. Sagmiller, *We Can Do It!* 19–20.

13. See Andrew Hutchison, "Further Background Information on Ronnie, the Bren Gun Girl."

14. See *Geni.com*, "Ronnie, the Bren Gun Girl."

15. "Ronnie, the Bren Gun Girl," Memoir Films.

16. Sherna Berger Gluck, *Rosie the Riveter Revisited*, 163.

17. Gluck, *Rosie the Riveter Revisited*, 164.

18. Gluck, *Rosie the Riveter Revisted*, 164–65.

19. Gluck, *Rosie the Riveter Revisted*, 170.

BIBLIOGRAPHY

101 Squadron. "The Story of the US Navy Ventura PV-1 28736." Available at http://www.101nisquadron.org/cairn-projects/the-story-of-us-navy -ventura-pv-1-28736/. Accessed 16 August 2018.

Aaseng, Nathan. *Navajo Code Talkers.* New York: Walker and Company, 1992.

Airforce Magazine. "Red Tails, the Tuskegee Airman in Photos," 18 March 2016. Available at http://www.airforcemag.com/Features/Pages/2016 /March%202016/Red-Tails-the-Tuskegee-Airmen-in-Photos.aspx. Accessed 16 August 2018.

American Battlefield Trust. "American Revolution—FAQs." Available at https://www.battlefield.org/learn/articles/american-revolution-faqs. Accessed 6 November 2018.

Anderson, Joseph Hyalmar. "My Service Diary." Unpublished. Copy in author's possession.

Asahina, Robert. *Just Americans: How Japanese Americans Won a War at Home and Abroad; The Story of the 100th Battalion/442nd Regimental Combat Team in World War II.* New York: Gotham Books, 2006.

Atwood, Kathryn J. *Women Heroes of World War II: 26 Stories of Espionage, Resistance, and Rescue.* Chicago: Chicago Review, 2011.

Bernstein, Alison. *American Indians and World War II: Toward a New Era in Indian Affairs.* Norman, OK: University of Oklahoma Press, 1991.

"The Bill of Rights: A Transcription." Available at https://www.archives .gov/founding-docs/bill-of-rights-transcript. Accessed 7 August 2018.

Botel, Ruth. "Fishermen Watch Scope Sink at Sea." *North Island Gazette,* 8 June 2005.

Botel, Ruth. "Plane Lost at Lawn Point during WWII." *North Island Gazette,* 1 June 2005.

Braddon, Russell. *Nancy Wake: SOE's Greatest Heroine.* Gloucestershire, UK: Stroud, 2010. Kindle.

Bush, George H. W. "Remarks to World War II Veterans and Families in Honolulu, Hawaii," 7 December 1991. *The American Presidency Project.* Available at http://www.presidency.ucsb.edu/ws/?pid=20316. Accessed 8 August 2018.

Chapelle, Dickey. *What's a Woman Doing Here? A Reporter's Report on Herself.* New York: William and Morrow, 1962.

CNN.com. "Navajo code talkers honored after 56 years." Available at http://edition.cnn.com/2001/US/07/26/code.talkers/index.html. Accessed 31 July 2018.

Colman, Penny. *Where the Action Was: Women War Correspondents in World War II.* New York: Crown Books, 2002.

Contrails. Official newsletter of the Royal Canadian Air Force 101st Squadron. Available at http://www.101nisquadron.org. Accessed 16 August 2018.

Crost, Lyn. *Honor by Fire: Japanese Americans at War in Europe and the Pacific.* Novato, CA: Presidio Press, 1994.

Davis, Benjamin O. Jr. *Benjamin O. Davis, Jr.: American: An Autobiography.* Washington, DC: Smithsonian, 1991.

Defense POW/MIA Accounting Agency. "Past Conflicts." Available at http://www.dpaa.mil/Our-Missing/Past-Conflicts/. Accessed 16 August 2018.

Densho Encyclopedia. "Rescue of the Lost Battalion." Available at http://encyclopedia.densho.org/Rescue_of_the_Lost_Battalion/. Accessed 7 August 2018.

Dickinson, Emily. *The Poems of Emily Dickinson: Reading Edition.* R.W. Franklin, ed. Cambridge, MA: The Belknap Press, 1999.

Divine, Jay. *Combat Engineer, Pacific Theater: Daily Life in an Army Construction Battalion in World War II.* Self-published. Xlibris, 2016. Kindle.

Dunlap, Tiare. "Rosie the Riveter at 95: Woman Who Inspired WWII Poster Was Lost to History for 7 Decades."*People,* 7 September 2016. Available at http://people.com/celebrity/rosie-the-riveter-meet-the -woman-who-inspired-the-iconic-poster/. Accessed 6 November 2018.

Educator Resources of the National Archives. "Black Soldiers in the US

Military during the Civil War." Available at https://www.archives.gov /education/lessons/blacks-civil-war. Accessed 16 August 2018.

Evans, Redd, and John Jacob Loeb. "Rosie the Riveter." *International Lyrics Playground.* Available at http://lyricsplayground.com/alpha/songs/r /rosietheriveter.shtml. Accessed 30 April 2018.

Fischer, David Hackett. *Liberty and Freedom: A Visual History of America's Founding Ideas.* Oxford: Oxford University Press, 2004.

Fletcher, Marvin E. *America's First Black General: Benjamin O. Davis, Sr., 1880–1970.* Lawrence, KS: University Press of Kansas, 1989.

Geni.com. "Ronnie, the Bren Gun Girl." Available at https://www.gen i.com/people/Ronnie-the-Bren-Gun-Girl/6000000031038807205. Accessed 31 July 2018.

GlobalSecurity.org. "7th Squadron, 10th Cavalry Regiment." Available at http://www.globalsecurity.org/military/agency/army/7-10cav.htm. Accessed 8 August 2018.

Gluck, Sherna Berger. *Rosie the Riveter Revisited: Women, the War and Social Change.* Boston: G. K. Hall, 1987.

Harry S. Truman Presidential Library and Museum. "Desegregation of the Armed Forces." Available at https://www.trumanlibrary.org/whistle stop/study_collections/desegregation/large/index.php?action=bg. Accessed 16 August 2018.

Hartmann, Susan M. *The Home Front and Beyond: American Women in the 1940s.* Boston: Twayne Publishers, 1982.

History.com. "American Women in World War II." Available at http:// www.history.com/topics/world-war-ii/american-women-in-world -war-ii. Accessed 30 April 2018.

Hutchison, Andrew. "Further Background Information on Ronnie, the Bren Gun Girl." *Andrew Hutchison: Artist.* Available at http://www .andrewhutchison.com/Ronnie_The_Bren_Gun_Girl/ Ronnie_The _Bren_Gun_Girl_Further_Details.html. Accessed 6 November 2018.

Kartchner, Bertha. *Memories of Hyalmar Anderson.* Unpublished manu- script.

Knox, Nelson R. Jr. *Combat Engineer: A World War 2 Memoir.* Bennington, Vermont: Merriam Press, 2015. Kindle.

Lee, Ulysses. *The Employment of Negro Troops.* Washington, DC: US Army Center of Military History, 1966. Available at https://history.army .mil/books/wwii/. Accessed 6 November 2018.

McPhate, Mike. "Joseph Medicine Crow, Tribal War Chief and Historian Dies at 102." *New York Times*, 4 April 2016. Available at https://www.nytimes.com/2016/04/05/us/joseph-medicine-crow-tribal-war-chief-and-historian-dies-at-102.html. Accessed 16 August 2018.

Medicine Crow, Joseph. *Counting Coup: Becoming a Crow Chief on the Reservation and Beyond.* Washington, DC: National Geographic, 2006.

———. *From the Heart of the Crow Country: The Crow Indians' Own Stories.* 1st ed. New York: Orion Books, 1992.

Memoir Films. "Ronnie, the Bren Gun Girl." YouTube.com. Available at https://www.youtube.com/watch?v=-E0KvWve-9g. Accessed 16 August 2018.

Mick Joffe Caricatures. "Nancy Wake, the White Mouse." Available at http://www.mickjoffe.com/Nancy_Wake. Accessed 13 August 2011.

Mill, John Stuart. *The Contest in America.* Reprinted from Fraser's Magazine. Boston: Little, Brown and Company, 1862.

Minahan, James. *Ethnic Groups of the Americas: An Encyclopedia.* Santa Barbara, CA: ABC-CLIO, 2013.

Minnesota History Center. "Women in the Military: World War II—Overview." Available at https://libguides.mnhs.org/wwii_women. Accessed 4 November 2018.

National World War II Museum. "African Americans in World War II: Fighting for a Double Victory." Available at https://www.national-ww2museum.org/sites/default/files/2017-07/african-americans.pdf. Accessed 31 July 2018.

Naval History and Heritage Command. "Navajo Code Talkers: World War II Fact Sheet." Available at https://www.history.navy.mil/research/library/online-reading-room/title-list-alphabetically/n/code-talkers.html. Accessed 30 April 2018.

Navy Life: The Official Blog of the US Navy. "The POW/MIA Table: A Place Setting for One, a Table for All." Available at http://navylive.dodlive.mil/2014/10/06/the-powmia-table-a-place-setting-for-one-a-table-for-all/comment-page-1/. Accessed 16 August 2018.

Nez, Chester. *Code Talker: The First and Only Memoir by One of the Original Navajo Code Talkers of WWII.* New York: Berkeley Caliber, 2011.

Norman, Michael, and Elizabeth Norman. *Tears in the Darkness: The Story of the Bataan Death March and Its Aftermath.* New York: Farrar, Straus, and Giroux, 2009.

Parker, Joni L. "Nisei Soliders in WWII: The Campaign in the Vosges Mountains." Master's thesis, US Army Command and General Staff College, 1994. Available at http://www.dtic.mil/dtic/tr/fulltext/u2 /a284556.pdf. Accessed 16 August 2018.

Pergrin, David E. and Eric M. Hammel. *First Across the Rhine: The 291st Engineer Combat Battalion in France, Belgium, and Germany.* St. Paul, MN: Zenith Press, 2006. First published 1989 by Pacifica Press (Pacifica, CA).

Personal Justice Denied: Report of the Commission on Wartime Relocation and Internment of Civilians. Washington, DC: US Government Printing Office, 1982–1983. Available at https://www.archives.gov/research /japanese-americans/justice-denied. Accessed 8 August 2018.

Sagmiller, Girard. *We Can Do It! A Rosie the Riveter Story, A Biography of My Mom: One Women's Story of Her Generation during World War II and Working as a Real-Life "Rosie the Riveter."* Self-published.

Shilling, Mikel. *Silent Heroes: The Story of the 284th Engineer Combat Battalion During World War II.* Self-published, 2017. Kindle.

Spinner, Jackie. "Remembering 'Fearless' War Photographer, Dickey Chapelle." *Columbia Journalism Review*, 16 November 2015. Available at https://www.cjr.org/united_states_project/dickey_chapelle_female _correspondent_killed_in_combat.php. Accessed 16 August 2018.

Sterner, C. Douglas. *Go for Broke: The Nisei Warriors of World War II Who Conquered Germany, Japan, and American Bigotry.* Clearfield, UT: American Legacy Historical Press, 2008.

Steward, T. G. *Buffalo Soldiers: The Colored Regulars in the United States Army.* New York: Dover, 2014. First published 1904 by A.M.E. Book Concern (Philadelphia).

Think Defence. "UK Military Bridging—Equipment (The Bailey Bridge)," January 8, 2012. Available at https://www.thinkdefence .co.uk/2012/01/uk-military-bridging-equipment-the-bailey-bridge/. Accessed 7 August 2018.

Vitello, Paul. "Nancy Wake, Proud Spy and Nazi Foe, Dies at 98." *New York Times*, 13 August 2011. Available at https://www.nytimes.com /2011/08/14/world/europe/14wake.html. Accessed 6 November 2018.

Waller, Jane, and Michael Vaughan-Rees. *Women in Wartime: The Role of Women's Magazines 1939–1945*. London: Macdonald Optima, 1990.

Weatherford, Doris. *American Women during World War II: An Encyclopedia*. London: Routledge, 2009.

White House. "Remarks by the President in a Ceremony Honoring the Navajo Code Talkers" (press release), 26 July 2001. Available at https://georgewbush-whitehouse.archives.gov/news/releases/2001/07/20010726-5.html. Accessed 16 August 2018.

Wilkey, Landon. "Asbestos Suits and Combat Boots: Engineer Aviation Fire Fighting Platoons of the United States Eight Air Force." Capstone paper, Utah State University, May 2016.

Willcke, Von Holger. "The 'Beer Bridge' Is Still Famous Today." *General-Anzeiger*, 3 March 2015.

IMAGE CREDITS

All images are used by permission unless otherwise noted.

Page 5: Pat Patton. Courtesy of the Patton Family.

Page 32: Nancy Wake. Public domain. Wikimedia.

Page 47: Joseph Hyalmar Anderson. Courtesy of the Anderson family.

Page 59: "Presidential Medal of Freedom recipient Joseph Medicine Crow shows a drum during a reception for recipients and their families in the Blue Room of the White House on Aug. 12, 2009." Taken by an employee of the Executive Office of the President of the United States. A work of the US federal government. Public domain. Wikimedia Commons.

Page 71: Dickey Chapelle covering Operation Inland Seas. Wisconsin Historical Society.

Page 99: Navajo Code Talkers. "Corporal Henry Bake, Jr., (left) and Private First Class George H. Kirk, Navajo Indians serving with a Marine Signal Unit, operate a portable radio set in a clearing they've just hacked in the dense jungle close behind the front lines." Image in public domain. Obtained at National Archives. Taken 9/18/1947.

Page 123: Purple Heart Battalion. "Awaiting orders to detrain at Camp Shelby, a quartet of Japanese-Americans swing out to the accompaniment of a Hawaiian ukulele." Library of Congress. Public domain. Taken June 1943.

Page 133: Combat Engineers. "Members of 2nd Battalion, 11th Infantry, cross the river at Dornot, France." Public domain. Wikimedia Commons.

Page 147: African Americans. "Photograph shows several Tuskegee airmen. Front row, left to right: unidentified airman; Jimmie D. Wheeler (with goggles); Emile G. Clifton (cloth cap) San Francisco, CA, Class 44-B. Standing left to right: Ronald W. Reeves (cloth cap) Washington, DC, Class 44-G; Hiram Mann (leather cap); Joseph L. 'Joe' Chineworth (wheel cap) Memphis, TN, Class 44-E; Elwood T. Driver? Los Angeles, CA, Class 44-A; Edward 'Ed' Thomas (partial view); Woodrow W. Crockett (wheel cap); at Ramitelli, Italy, March 1945. (Source: Tuskegee Airmen 332nd Fighter Group pilots.)" Library of Congress. Public domain. Toni Frissell (1907–1988), photographer. Taken March 1945.

Page 160. Rosie the Riveter. "Riveter at work on Consolidated bomber, Consolidated Aircraft Corp., Fort Worth, Texas." Howard R. Hollem, photographer. Taken October 1942. Public domain. Library of Congress.

INDEX